Soul Sisters

Soul Sisters

DEVOTIONS FOR AND FROM AFRICAN AMERICAN, LATINA, AND ASIAN WOMEN

SUZAN JOHNSON COOK

*Former U.S. 3rd Ambassador-at-Large
for International Religious Freedom*

A TARCHERPERIGEE BOOK

tarcherperigee

An imprint of Penguin Random House LLC
375 Hudson Street
New York, New York 10014

Scripture quotations marked NIV are from the *Holy Bible, New International Version*® NIV®. Copyright © 1973, 1978, 1984, 2011 by Biblica, Inc.® Used by permission of Biblica, Inc.® All rights reserved worldwide.

Scripture quotations marked CEV are from the *Contemporary English Version*. Copyright © 1991, 1992, 1995 by American Bible Society. Used by permission of American Bible Society.

Scripture passages marked NLT are taken from the *Holy Bible, New Living Translation*. Copyright ©1996, 2004, 2007, 2013 by Tyndale House Foundation. Used by permission of Tyndale House Publishers, Inc., Carol Stream, Illinois 60188. All rights reserved.

Scripture quotations marked MSG are from *The Message*. Copyright © 1993, 1994, 1995, 1996, 2000, 2001, 2002 by Eugene H. Peterson. Used by permission of Tyndale House Publishers, Inc.

Scripture quotations marked KJV are from the *Holy Bible, King James Version*.

Scripture quotations marked NKJV are from the *New King James Version*®. Copyright © 1982 by Thomas Nelson. Used by permission of Thomas Nelson. All rights reserved.

Scripture quotations marked HCSB are taken from the *Holman Christian Standard Bible*. Copyright © 1999, 2000, 2002, 2003 by Holman Bible Publishers. Used by permission of Holman Bible Publishers.

Tarcher and Perigee are registered trademarks, and the colophon is a trademark of Penguin Random House LLC.

Most Tarcher/Penguin books are available at special quantity discounts for bulk purchase for sales promotions, premiums, fund-raising, and educational needs. Special books or book excerpts also can be created to fit specific needs. For details, write: SpecialMarkets@penguinrandomhouse.com.

eBook ISBN 9781101983539

Library of Congress Cataloging-in-Publication Data
Names: Johnson Cook, Suzan D. (Suzan Denise), 1957– contributor, compiler.
Title: Soul sisters : devotions for and from African American, Latina, and Asian Women / Suzan Johnson Cook.
Description: New York : Jeremy P. Tarcher-Penguin, 2016.
Identifiers: LCCN 2015048811 | ISBN 9781585429479 (paperback)
Subjects: LCSH: Women—Religious life. | Devotional literature.
Classification: LCC BV4527 .S6485 2016 | DDC 204/.4082—dc23

Printed in the United States of America
1 3 5 7 9 10 8 6 4 2

Book design by Elke Sigal

To all women, anywhere and everywhere, who dare to dream, to share, and to care, and who believe in the power of prayer. It is your story—our stories—that give honor and glory to God, and allow healing to take place for so many sisters around the world.

Thank you for all the help and healing you've allowed to happen in and through you. Thank you for sharing and for daring to care.

FOREWORD

Soul Sisters—they come into your life in mysterious ways. They may be childhood friends, actual blood relatives, or strangers who bonded while going through a similar crisis. This female camaraderie, this instant trust and admiration—it's a beautiful phenomenon that I have had the blessing of experiencing with many women throughout my life, and the honor of sharing with Ambassador Suzan Johnson Cook. In a very short time we became close friends, business partners, and steadfast supporters—*hermanas*.

We first met at the Union Theological Seminary in New York City, where she spoke at a breakfast for Women of Faith. Sujay, as she is affectionately known by friends and colleagues all around the world, was then the U.S. 3rd Ambassador-at-Large for International Religious Freedom. Notwithstanding the impressive title, Sujay was just a warm, gregarious lady who was there to inspire and connect with the women attending the event. Through her stories, she captured the audience from the stage. I was deeply moved and followed a calling in my heart to introduce myself and say hello. Now, a few years later, I am humbled with the privilege of writing this foreword for *Soul Sisters*.

Actually, creating the sacred space and fertile ground where soul sisters are born is a very big part of my life's work. My nonprofit organization, Milagros Day Worldwide, is dedicated to empowering survivors of domestic violence and childhood trauma through leadership coaching and mentorship. Our tag line is "Turning Abuse Into Success"—and the only way to achieve that mission is through our multicultural community of sisterhood.

Reading *Soul Sisters* is like looking in the mirror and seeing our deepest inner fears and judgments dissolved. It is a knowing that through all our mistakes and our doubts we are okay—we are doing our best, and we are worthy of our own respect.

It is saying to our daughters *and* to our sons that they have a voice and we hear them!

Reading the stories in *Soul Sisters* reminds us that as we age, faith is our fountain of youth, and faith is what keeps us balanced. This book gives us permission to relax and enjoy the ride of life that is filled with laughter and loss, legacy and love—because through it all we will always have the comfort and the encouragement of our Soul Sisters.

Dawn Diaz
April 2016

Dawn Diaz is a corporate trainer, life coach, motivational speaker, retired New York City Fire Department captain/paramedic, and coauthor of Building on Greatness, the Courage to Thrive. *She is the CEO of the Rescue Coaching Institute, founder of Milagros Day Worldwide, and creator of the iconic Annual Brooklyn Bridge Mother's Day Walk and Family Festival.*

ACKNOWLEDGMENTS

First and foremost, I thank God for the privilege and blessing of being given the gift of writing and for the ability to bring women together in person, on paper, in prayer, and in politics in both the public and private spheres.

God gives the talent; still, someone has to grant the opportunity. My literary agent, Lois de la Haba, along with Joel Fotinos—whom I refer to as the dynamic duo—Andrew, and the Tarcher Penguin family have given me opportunity.

I'd also like to thank Lindsey Payne, a young woman who helped me to compile this book and keep my many moving parts on track this past year.

I wish to thank Rev. Olivia M. Cloud, my Delta Sigma Theta sorority sister; and Adrienne Ingrum, who reminded me of her special gifts, warmth, and talent. Thank you to all the contributors, editors, and eyes that have peered through, and the anointed hands that have touched, written, and edited these blessed pages.

And as always, I thank my guys—my sons, Sam and Chris, and Ron—who always allowed me to be woman in a household of men. I wouldn't have it any other way.

And to all my prayer partners, Merc being the chief one, who have prayed me to and through, and looked out for me even when I didn't and couldn't pray for myself, or know who to look out for, thank you.

My heart, passion, and compassion for the past three decades of my life have been devoted to helping women amplify their voices and bring healing to the world through women. *Soul Sisters* does just that.

Every contributor in this book is extra special to me. You have blessed and honored me with your presence in these pages, which will outlive each of us and reach with our collective hands into the hearts of so many sisters.

CONTENTS

INTRODUCTION

Rarely do we get to write about, talk about, or display our passion in words, witness, and writing for the whole world to experience. I've been blessed to do all three. I have been most passionate about bringing women of faith and women of color together, to be transparent and to help one another in word, thought, and deed. Often I host Destiny Circles with women in my living room (see *Becoming a Woman of Destiny*, New York: Tarcher Penguin, 2011), and I begin each session with the Woman of Destiny Prayer:

> God,
> Thank you for creating me woman,
> Thank you for teaching me how to give and receive love
> Please go before me, to show me the way,
> Please go behind me, to push me with your divine touch.
> Please watch over me that I may be covered in your
>   unconditional love
> Most of all, please give me wisdom to walk the paths that
>   you have blazed and ordained for me, and to know the
>   difference between right and wrong.
> I invite you inside me that I may have your anointing
> I seek you everywhere that I may know your fullness
> Teach me to make wise choices in every area of my life.
> Surround me with and keep me in the midst of other wise
>   women

Give me the clarity to share the wisdom I have to impart
To women who seek to be wise themselves
Thank you for creating me woman
I am blessed and highly favored
I am a woman of destiny
I am seeking Divine decisions
I am destined for greatness
   From *Becoming a Woman of Destiny*

I also host ProVoice/ProVoz monthly national Gatherings for women leaders, to amplify the voices of women. We have a most memorable time. It's a "safe space" for women, where hearts and minds meet souls, where conversation meets celebration. And it is in and through the shared prayers and cares that something almost magical happens.

Many of the women from my gatherings and close friendships have contributed writings to this book, and we hope that the enchanted experience in our gatherings can be replicated through reading these pages. May you feel and experience, through writing, what we experience when we are together: affection, connection, protection, embrace, soul, and solace—and here it is, in *Soul Sisters*, through thoughts, prayers, and literature.

Touching a woman's soul takes someone with vision, insight, and concern about the *soul* to invite us into the literary world, as authors and editors, to facilitate the experience. That happened with the compilation of this book: *Soul Sisters: Devotions for and from African American, Latina, and Asian Women*. More than forty women from diverse cultures and races have come together, in shared prayers and cares, as women of faith seeking to connect with other women of faith. The expressions written herein are shared from the deepest places of sisters' souls—a must-read, if I do say so myself.

We are sharing our stories because we understand that some days a woman just needs some strength and devotion, not strife or division, and she doesn't have all day to "get there." The boast doesn't have to be a long treatise, but it must be strong. And sometimes a sister just needs that spiritual reinforcement to come from another sister.

As I compiled this book, I declared my candidacy for the U.S. House of Representatives, from New York's Thirteenth Congressional District. I am so grateful for the sisters who came together to launch me with a prayer/faith breakfast, because they knew I would need to lean and depend on my faith continually.

"Give us this day our daily bread," says the Lord's Prayer. *Soul Sisters* can give you a measure of what you need daily. On the day you need to be reminded to laugh, there's a devotion for that. If you need a quick reminder about the power of faith, there are devotions for that. When you are dealing with loss, whether great or small, the book has inspired writings for that as well. When you experience love, *Soul Sisters* has shared words to reflect that experience as well.

I am particularly drawn to the section called "Letters to our Sons," because I raised two sons in this twenty-first century; they are now men. I cover them daily in prayer, that they may be bathed in honor, devotion, and dignity.

These are all experienced themes, which have led to the devotions that nearly fifty sisters wish to share with you. May you be blessed by them.

❧

At about age sixteen, I wanted to share something deep and personal with my mother, but I couldn't quite find the words, courage, confidence, or the way to convey it. I wrote her a letter. My missive was the breakthrough I had hoped for as a teen trying to get my message across to an adult.

My mom reacted to my words as a mother who loved and cared, but most of all, as one who heard and felt me. She would continue to hear me over the years, even as I evolved and matured. Our relationship experienced a major shift as I was about to enter young womanhood. It was a feeling of deep love and trust that propelled me forward, knowing that I was not alone, nor would I have to face uncertainties without the "cover" of a mother's love.

After my parents had passed away, I discovered letters they had written to one another: love letters as they were dating, as young adults, and well into marriage. The joy and understanding I received from that glimpse into their history and their deep and abiding loyalty and love for one another became a model of what I wanted and hoped for, in men, in marriage, and in motherhood.

I wanted readers to have a similar experience, and so you will find letters in this book—liberating letters, and stories, and blessings, and "how I made it over" testimonies. Many of the women contributing to this work have left legacies for the sons and daughters and other men and women they love in their writing.

Compiling *Soul Sisters* reminds me of a similar experience I had in 1988, when I was blessed to edit *Sister to Sister: Devotions for and from African American Women*, Volume 1 (Judson Press), a collection of thematic devotions for and from a cross section of African American women. The book contained stories, some in letter and other prose forms and genres, from forty-eight Black women who had been in my life from childhood through adulthood. They shared the truth of how women, Black Christian women, had made it through some trying times. We found that healing came through sharing our stories; joy also came. From reflections about being alone, to recountings about being celebrated collectively, the stories and the readers' reactions to them were riveting and liberating, joyous and freeing.

I wanted to broaden and expand that vision of success. *Soul Sisters* comes from women of color, multicultural women, finding common and not-so-common ground to navigate through twenty-first-century waters. We tread these territories as females of faith, courage, and color, and as global citizens who've learned how to enlarge our landscape, crossing ethnic, racial, and geographical lines, to understand that sisters with soul are worldwide.

I have found in sharing real-life, "from the heart" stories and devotions that liberation—true freedom—happens for women. *Sister to Sister* shared a woman's story of losing an adult child, that helped grieving families, and the parent who penned it, to move forward. There were the stories of feeling lonely as a "new kid" on the block, and other women coming to the rescue, to welcome them in. *Sister to Sister* became a bestseller because women needed to share and hear from real-life women about real-life, relevant issues.

On my amazing journey as U.S. 3rd Ambassador-at-Large for International Religious Freedom, I had 199 countries as part of my portfolio. As I traveled around the world, more than meeting the famous and the infamous, I was captured and captivated by the eyes, the silent voices, and the strength of the souls of women I met.

More often than not, I had diplomatic engagements with male governmental leaders, but I had my greatest spiritual experiences during those after hours. That's when I heard from women who had been victims of war, women who had led peace efforts, and women who had helped to nurture other women.

During those times, sister-to-sister, female-to-female, we shared from the heart. We shared things they had prayed for, and things they wanted us to continue to pray for. How glorious were those moments! It was during those opportunities that the seed impregnated in my spirit to somehow address and amplify the *souls* of my *sisters*.

Then in 2013, the Lord gave me a vision for bringing women together—to amplify, multiply, and fortify our voices and to provide a forum to gather, celebrate, motivate, and share our stories. Exactly one year later, I heard an audiotape during a memorial service for the late actress Ruby Dee, "Calling All Women," in which she rhythmically declared that women of all nationalities needed to come together. Thereafter, the ProVoice/ProVoz movement was born, and marked by a gathering of women in the art gallery of the Adam Clayton Powell Jr. State Office Building, in Harlem, New York. The movement began with a dance to Cindy Trimm's poem "I Am."

The hundred or so women assembled there clapped, sang, laughed, applauded, threw the "power sign" up, giggled, and teared up as they grasped the spirit and souls and connected with every other sister in that room. The inaugural movement was an opportunity—not to have an agenda, but rather to *be* the agenda. It was for, about, and *by* women. That first meeting was sharing out of our diversity and our commonalities and the multitude of hats we wear and hopes we embrace—business, dreams, screams, hard times, good times, and "I don't know" times. For hours, we shared and we cared out of the wealth of sisterhood.

Many of the women who shared in the experience that day were invited to write for this new volume of devotions. The wisdom and insight they bring are both timeless and ageless. The release of this devotional comes at a significant milestone, as this is the twenty-fifth anniversary of *Sister to Sister*, Volume 1. Because of that work, healing has happened for so many through the years as they have thumbed through its pages.

Soul Sisters is compelling, lively, liberating, and luscious. Read and discover something that another woman did or did not do that can help you in your situation. I call it Life 101.

Life is a journey with a clear starting point, but we never know the end of the story, or how it may veer to the left or the right. The Marys and Marthas and Salomes of the Bible did not know how the story would end with their teacher, Jesus, but they kept moving, armed with their spices. The women in this collection tell you in real time what it's been like to stay the course or to pick up where someone left off. Some of them share what it's like surviving in the midst of something. That's the spice we bring.

This is just the beginning. Be blessed by the rest. The blessed of us must help the rest of us.

I have found that in my three decades of ministry, broadly and globally defined, it is through sharing our stories that we find healing, and uncover and discover our soul's secrets. May the heartfelt experiences offered in these pages be guideposts along your life path.

Blessings on Your Journey, My Sister,
Ambassador Sujay

RAISING THEM RIGHT

Direct your children onto the right path,
and when they are older, they will not leave it.

PROVERBS 22:6, NLT

I did what was done to me. I thought my mother and father were in-ordinately strict when they wouldn't let me go out on a date just be-cause some boy had asked me. If I wanted to hang out with a new friend, they had to know all about the person's family—parents, where they lived, and so forth. It was a nuisance then, but now I see it as a blessing. Their inquisitions saved me from dangers unknowable and unseen by my young eyes.

As unyielding as I thought my parents were, I became the same kind of mother. My sons always wanted to bring friends home. I loved having their friends over, but I insisted on knowing about each of them. Where does he live? Who are his parents? I asked of them all the questions that had once frustrated me as a teen. After I became a mother, I understood my parents' inquisitiveness as responsible parenting.

Many of today's parents, especially mothers, blur the lines of parental authority, opting to be their child's friend. Growing up, there were many times I was angry with my mother because of a decision she'd made regarding what I could or could not do. I know it wasn't her goal to make me angry, but I don't think she spent a lot of time stressing about it, either. She wasn't trying to be one of my girlfriends, though I know that she was the best girlfriend I could ever have.

My mother had her partner, my father, as her teammate to help her navigate unknown parental waters. But today many mothers are trying to figure it out alone. According to some statistical estimates, nearly 70 percent of African American children live in single-parent households. The same applies to over 50 percent of Native American children and over 40 percent of Latino children. Black, Latina, and Native American mothers are coping with the very real stress of solo parenting.

This brings to mind a young woman who was in a store parking lot yelling at her three-year-old son for doing something, whatever it was, that three-year-olds do. She screamed at the top of her lungs, calling him dumb, with a few expletives sprinkled in between. What most people who witnessed the episode saw was an unfit single mother with three children. But there was more to that young woman with the rambunctious three-year-old, an eighteen-month-old in a stroller, and a nine-month-old baby on her hip.

There's no excuse for talking to a child that way. But it's just possible she was a mother afraid a car would hit her son. And if he got in harm's way she wouldn't be able to reach him quickly because her hands were already full with his two sisters. It's also possible that she was frustrated at her condition, having three very young children and trying to hold down a household all alone. It's possible that she vented her frustration with absent fathers on their very present children, whom she was left to rear.

That parking lot scenario makes one wonder, What if Mary had gotten frustrated with Jesus and called Him dumb? Mary had the benefit of knowing she had been given a gift. She had a mother/sister to affirm that for her. She was also blessed with a father for her son.

But what of all the mothers who have no one to explain to them that each of her children is a gift? Mary birthed the Son of God, but so many other mothers have birthed potential greatness unknowingly. And because they did not know, they could not nurture.

It's time for enlightened sisters to take another look around, to open our eyes and see the frustrated young mother for who she really is—for what she has and for what she lacks. See her as a young woman who still needs to be mothered, even as she raises children of her own. Help her to see the value of the gifts she has birthed.

Help her to develop the tools she needs to raise them right—to know who her children's friends are, and who their parents are and where they live. Walk beside her to know the difference between parenting and friendship, that there's a line that should not be crossed for many, many years.

I did what was done to me. Perhaps too many young mothers, like the one in the store parking lot, only did what was done to them, as well.

Soul Sisters

LETTERS TO OUR SONS

Reflections & *The Mother of Sons*

I Release You in Love
DR. SUZAN JOHNSON COOK

Blessed for the Journey
ELIZABETH MURRAY

Someday We'll Be Together . . . Again
LUCIA McBATH

Your Name Is Caleb, Your Name Is Faith
LATONYA ELLIS

Reflections ❧ *The Mother of Sons*

Boy, oh boy. I am the mother of sons. I had always prayed for sons. Had I started having babies earlier in life, I might have had the four that I really wanted. Nevertheless, God blessed me with two healthy sons. And I am a mother made for boys. They met their match, and I met mine.

Their dad named them, but I carried them. Each gave me nine months—yes, nine months—of morning sickness. In spite of that, it was a joy to carry them and it has been absolutely terrific being their mom.

I was a senior pastor at the time I carried them, so they were born into and raised in the church. I remember so well their movements as I would preach; the oldest loved it when gospel music was played or sung.

I've enjoyed every stage and season, from kissing their boo-boos to being a soccer mom and driving them to the string of practices for teams that I had lined up.

At this writing, I just got off the phone with the eldest, Samuel. He is a college graduate who just entered medical school to pursue his dream. He followed me with all of my dreams. Now it's his turn to see what this world has to offer—and what he has to offer the world. What a moment to see him receive his "white coat" that indicates you are officially a "med student" and watch him take the Hippocratic oath. Yes, I cried. I've done what the Lord required in terms of provision, protection, and parenting. And now, Sam will step into and onto the world platform, bringing the knowledge and gifts he has to share.

Our younger son, Christopher, is a junior at Princeton University, an athlete/scholar—disciplined, dedicated, delightful. Phone conversations and hundreds of text messages are now more meaningful as he learns to appreciate the sacrifices that have been made on his behalf.

As I compile this devotional, so much is going in the world: the ISIS crisis; the ongoing racism and violence in America; and the disgust, disrespect, and disregard for Black men and men of color. Some days I wish I could hold my sons and just rock them in my arms as I did when they were younger and smaller, but now I must release them to the world into which they were born and show my love for them through texts, calls, e-mails, prayers, and letters.

As a mother two of sons, there are so many times a day that I want to leave my thoughts, lessons, and love with them. I started writing letters to them when they were born. Recently I came across a letter I'd written to them during an overseas trip and put into one of those tubes that are placed in the ocean in the event something happens. The tube goes into the sea and makes its way toward home. As my eldest graduated from college, I also created a photo life journal, with letters interspersed, so that one day when he is reminiscing, he'll have letters and photos from his mom.

Both sons now have girlfriends, women with whom they spend a lot of time. I can only imagine that it will just be a matter of time before they marry and have families, so this is also my rite of passage, as I move over to allow new maturity to enter their lives. The letters will help me to know that I can speak not only with my mouth but also with my heart and soul, shared prayers, and cares.

Being mothers of African American males in this nation, in this world, we raise them with a heap of love, so they'll never forget where they come from and can always return to loving homes and parents. Yet, we have to rear them with enough strength to be strong men, and to first know the strong roots from which they come—fathers and grandfathers, brothers and uncles, and pastors, who all had pride in who we are as a people, and whose we are, as children of God. These truths must be blended with the realities they face as men of color who are strong, smart, and capable of expressing the love they have received.

The world is not always ready for men of color to make such an incredible impact, or to have such international influence, or to excel as much in academics as they do in sports. So as mothers, we write, speak, tweet, text, or send Facebook messages to our sons on a daily basis. We try to mother rather than smother. But I must admit there are days when I fail miserably and I hug them as often as I can, because there's so much to say, to share, to tell.

They really don't know how many hours we stay awake, pretending to be asleep when they come home at a late hour. Nor do they realize that as mothers, we know the traps, the land mines, and the wars that have their names on them. And as mothers of Black and brown males, we already understand a system that's designed to take them if they get off the right path, or track them if they even look like they're about to fall. There's a hefty price. I now understand the phrase "blood, sweat, and tears." It took all of that for our forebears, and it still does, for us.

So we sing our lullabies to them while they are in our womb and as they grow into toddlers. We tuck them in at night with an extra dose of kisses when they are small, and then squeeze them with extra care as we send them off to school and camp.

We try hard to deal with their transitions to manhood as best we can. I must admit that I hug them so-o-o-o much. Both of my sons grew up and left about the same time, as they are a little more than two years apart in age. And yes, I've taught them the best life lessons I know—to be independent, to love God and their parents, to treat women with respect, to give back, to pay forward, and to do unto others as they would have others do unto them. But now I must trust

God and them to put those lessons into life's practices—to find their path and then walk, maybe even run to it, on it.

So this chapter, for me, is an opportunity for mothers of sons to collectively laugh, lament, learn, listen, leave legacies, gain some staying power, and even shed a tear or two, as we write to our sons in *this* generation.

Langston Hughes wrote the poem "Mother to Son" during the Black Renaissance. In the poem, the mother tells her son her life story, that "life ain't been no crystal stair. . . ." For most of us writing in this collection of devotions, life has not been crystal stairs, but many of us have cracked the "crystal ceilings," so this is not so much about us as it is about them.

The interesting thing about letters is that you don't know when or if they will be read, nor will you know what kind of impact they will have, if any. But write them we must, for our hearts are shared with those sons whom we love. They are filled with wisdom, warnings, and witness; signed, sealed, and delivered with love, in love. May you be blessed as you read these letters, and may our sons be blessed as they receive the messages contained therein.

What Shall I Tell Them?

When I was in college, I ran across a poem titled "What Shall I Tell My Children Who Are Black?" by Dr. Margaret Burroughs, cofounder of Chicago's DuSable Museum of African American History. The words Dr. Burroughs wrote resonated in my spirit even then, and stayed with me long after I married and became a mother, because I wanted my sons to understand the richness of their African American heritage. Black males face special challenges, and I wanted to give my sons the foundation they needed to make it in a world that is less than affirming to them.

Dr. Burroughs's poem embodies the meaning behind the mythical sankofa bird: that we hold on to the past as we move toward the future. The word sankofa is from the Akan language of Ghana; it encourages a people to go back and get what was once forgotten or lost. So much of contemporary culture denigrates Black men and has low expectations of them. I wanted my young Black boys to become men who would reach as high and as far as their enthusiasm and effort would carry them. I wanted them to understand that their heritage was not the negative stereotypes so often fed to us by the media; rather, their roots were those so elegantly articulated by Dr. Burroughs.

In the more than thirty years since I first read the poem, the two young men who are my sons—the younger halfway through Princeton and the older just having received his white coat for medical school—are strong Black men, educated in the best private schools and armed with love from their "village" and with knowledge of their heritage. They have applied themselves and are climbing the ladder of their success, and because they know from whence they have come, they are better equipped to know where they are going. They are now on their path.

I Release You in Love

DR. SUZAN JOHNSON COOK

Listen, my son! Listen, son of my womb!
Listen, my son, the answer to my prayers!
PROVERBS 31:2, NIV

Reared in the Black Church, with their mom as their pastor, now they must be released to the world, where I know racism and sexism and classism exist. It is the same world into which my mother released me. A few of the dynamics have changed, but it is still a world that every mother gives her child to, much like Hannah gave her son Samuel to the priest Eli, so that he could grow to the next level. As I let them go, I do so trusting that they received and felt enough love to prepare them for the not-so-loving times. . . . So here is my special message to them.

Dear sons, Sam and Chris:

I have loved you from the moment you came through me to the hands of two loving parents, your dad and me. We held each of you, cried, and thanked God for you at birth. My mother, whom you lovingly called Grandma Dot, lived to see both of you, and she stood over me as I gave birth to you. It was the happiest highlight of my life, to have our three generations connected in the same space.

You were birthed in love, dedicated at the altar in love, and reared in love. Now I release you—in love—to navigate your paths, to explore and contribute to this world, knowing that you can always come home.

The time has come for you to begin establishing your own homes. But I still love it when you come home and bring your friends, when you find space for them at our table, and when they want to spend the night. I'm excited that these experiences have passed from my generation to yours. It was the way I was raised, in an "all the way live" house.

I'm also glad that diversity has been a part of your growing-up experience. You moved five times in six years with me as I pursued my dreams. Now it's your turn to go after your own hearts' desires. You have been the sons of a pastor, a prayer warrior, and the sons of a diplomat. But most of all you are *our* sons.

No matter where life takes you, know that Dad and Mom love you. There is *nothing* you cannot share with me.

Remember where the important papers are, and know that we love you. Nothing can cause us to *stop* loving you. Honor God. Honor your parents. Honor and respect the men and women friends in your life.

Budget wisely. Don't overdo or overdue. When the cops say, "Stop!" stop. There will be women all over you and attracted to you. I know this because you are men they'd like to bring home to their parents.

Make wise choices. Be respectful. Be loyal. Be frugal. Be faithful. You have nothing to prove.

Know that there will be some tough and rough days. Life is not always easy, but believe me when I say from experience, that prayer and faith *will* get you through. As the song says, "We've come this far by faith."

Be blessed, my young warriors. The world has been waiting for you.

And you are READY.

With all my love,
Mom

Blessed for the Journey

ELIZABETH MURRAY

Sons are indeed a heritage from the Lord, the fruit of the
womb a reward.

PSALM 127:3, NRSV

I was a bit tardy arriving in this world on my
mother's due date, March 15. She was shocked
and exclaimed, "Oh, no!" when I arrived one
lovely Monday afternoon on April 1. This is
traditionally known as All Fools' Day, a day to
play pranks and jokes on everyone. You must
believe me when I tell you I had a challenging
childhood just admitting to my birthday, while
everyone else celebrated their special day with expectations of joy and
presents.

I went through life proving I was not a foolish person, but rather,
one who satisfactorily met goals that set me up for an upwardly mobile
lifestyle. Being a proud Black woman, I took on the task of being a
single mother of two young boys after my marriage ended in divorce.
My parents, from North and South Carolina, instilled in me the values
and tools I needed while financially taking care of the three of us. I was
always spiritually motivated, being brought up in the African Methodist Episcopal Zion Church; thus I had faith that I could bring up my
sons to be upright, solid, and productive members of any community.

Today I want to tell my sons what a joy it was to participate with them in the many community organizations with activities that emphasized strong values and that helped me shape their personalities. This involvement also affected my personal growth and allowed me to socially interact with a lot of influential people.

Working a full-time job, I enrolled at Fordham University at night while my sons were pursuing degrees at State University of New York at New Paltz and Marist College.

We shared and applied the educational lessons to our everyday lives as they afforded us comfortable lifestyles and careers, in banking, as a financial planner, and as a college administrator. We encouraged each other as Blacks to be independent thinkers and developed a quest for entrepreneurship. Sadly, we found it difficult to detach ourselves from the corporate world, which was topped with glass ceilings that blocked promotions we'd earned but couldn't seem to receive.

Not to be defeated, the three of us supplemented our jobs with accomplishments in other areas of our lives by applying the lessons learned through our higher-education courses, thereby realizing successes that could not be taken away from us. Proof positive it worked: I'm now looking forward to the influence I can have on my seven grandchildren and seven great-granddaughters.

To the grown men and grandfathers I call my sons, life allowed you to mature without being involved in a military war. You have, however, had to witness the war on crime in our Black neighborhoods, where Black-on-Black fatalities are way out of hand, and hopelessness and high unemployment are a way of life.

Both of you were fortunate to escape involvement in gangs, thus achieving my mission for you to become productive members of society. I'm so proud you two actively participated in rites-of-passage programs for young boys who are missing a father figure to guide them. It is necessary for each generation to elevate and to pass on knowledge that leads to favorable achievements. You were instrumental in giving these boys tools to build their self-esteem, which is a stepping-stone to any meaningful purpose in life. Being a role model for them has taught your own sons valuable lessons, which they understood as a basis of what it means to be a man. Thanks for offering "How to Develop Wealth and Prosper" seminars, which improve the community as a whole and give hope to young people who didn't have the opportunity to learn these important lessons at home.

Now that I'm a Medicare-eligible senior, I smile as I look back at my experiences and know that I'm blessed, for I'm confident that my journey so far has been productive and meaningful, and there was no joking or fooling around about it.

Someday We'll Be Together . . . Again

LUCIA McBATH

I thank my God every time I remember you.
PHILIPPIANS 1:3, NIV

Today is Sunday. As I sit on a plane this morning, staring out the window, I can't help but think of you, my sweet Jordan. It is funny, but I always feel a strong sense of comfort when I am in the air. Maybe it's because I feel closer to you and God when I'm thirty thousand feet high. Maybe it's because I envision you standing in the clouds with Jesus.

There is a great sense of serenity here above the clouds, but I can only imagine your peace, which is everlasting. I fully expect that when God calls me home, your face will be the first to greet me.

Are you happy to be in the arms of God? Sometimes, I wish I were with you, but then I realize I have too much to live for. For the first time I fully understand my purpose in life "for such a time as this."

When I look back over these past two and a half years since you were murdered, I marvel at how God answered my simple prayer that He would use the two of us for His purpose. I guess all the times I spiritually gave you back to God I never imagined I was preparing myself to give you physically over to God for a greater purpose.

I am so proud of who you have become in death as well as life. I am so proud that you loved others so deeply. I know this by the count-less stories people tell me. To see and know you through the eyes of others you had relationships with has been a wonderful gift. But the joy and unconditional love we shared as mother and son is my great-est gift of all.

Remember all the sunny summer days at the pool? Or the deep conversations about life and God we used to have as we rode in the car? Remember roller-skating with our homeschool group on Monday nights? I fondly remember your many boyhood sleepovers on the weekends and miss the bunches of boys who used to come over and eat me out of house and home.

I hope I gave you a good life full of love and respect. And I hope you know I am always your greatest cheerleader and number one fan. I hope you know how much I love you and that I am grateful for the seventeen years we had together.

I am now coming to understand why the Lord called you home. I've come to accept the purpose for which He is using you and me, and this gives me peace in moving forward.

Honey, I think about you every single day, and not a moment goes by that I do not feel your presence. Someday we will be together again, but until then I will continue to do the work to save as many lives as I can. I will continue to tell the world your story in hopes it will convince people to act so that no more people die by acts of gun violence.

Jordan, your death as well as your life matter to me and to the whole nation. I will always love you and I miss you immeasurably. Hold a spot in heaven for me, sweetie, because one day I'm coming home, too.

I love you from my soul,
Mom

Your Name Is Caleb, Your Name Is Faith

LaTONYA ELLIS

For I know the thoughts that I think toward you, saith the Lord, thoughts of peace and not of evil, to give you an expected end.

JEREMIAH 29:11, KJV

Dear son,

Today I kissed you and watched you board the bus that would transport you to the first day of your next journey in life—high school. I wanted to cling to you and not let you go, but I put up a brave front so that I wouldn't place a cloud over your big day.

Truthfully, I had great pain, fear, and anxiety about what you might encounter on the way to school. Would the kids be nice or would they be vicious? Would you be able to withstand the weight of negative peer pressure or would positive influences inspire you to blossom more than ever before? I'm sure these are the questions and concerns of a lot of parents. But my biggest concern was whether you would *live*. I doubt that is a question most parents have and I'm personally glad that they don't. But, son, when you have lost one teenage child to violence, it's a question that definitely haunts you as a parent.

Losing a child not only moves me to wonder about your future, but it also causes me to consider my own as a parent. As I question what awaits you in high school, I also have tough questions for myself. Have I done anything better or different with you than I did with your brother? Will God spare me the anguish and heartache this go-round? Can I trust and have faith that in the next few years I will be crying tears of joy at your graduation ceremony rather than tears of despair over a casket?

But let me tell you how God works. Just when I had questioned and had worried myself to the brink of a breakdown, a friend reminded me that you are *not* your brother. You are uniquely you and God had a specific plan for your life before you were even conceived. That plan started with your name, Caleb, which means "faith."

On September 19, 2012, at 2:53 P.M., our world forever changed. In the darkness of your brother's death, I couldn't see the way. How would I make it for myself, let alone muster up enough strength to raise you? But the faith that God placed within *you* was immediately activated, and your life light shone bright enough for the both of us to take the next part of our journey one step at a time.

Over the past four years, a lot has changed for both us. Yet God has placed an incomprehensible peace within us regarding DeMarcus's death. I have become a different person, and I hope a better parent— the kind of parent that you need to help guide you in life.

You have taught me temperance and patience (well, I'm still working on that one). You've taught me not to dwell on the negative, the bad, or the sad, but instead to be joy-filled. And we have taught each other to *live*, even though death has become such a strong reality.

I know you probably think I am weird when I just smile at you and pinch your cheek, but when I look at you I know you are truly my gift from God.

So as you start this new journey, you can be assured that the blood of Jesus covers you, and that your mom loves you to the moon and beyond. I'm very proud of the young man you have become and I know that you will do great things in life. And if you ever doubt it, read and meditate on Jeremiah 29:11: "For I know the thoughts that I think toward you, saith the Lord, thoughts of peace and not of evil, to give you an expected end."

Blessings and Love,
Mom

LETTERS TO OUR DAUGHTERS

Reflections & Mothers Raising Daughters

Reflections & Mothers Raising Daughters

Mothers have been accused of loving their sons while raising their daughters, especially African American mothers. As a mother of two sons, I must confess there may be some truth in the observation. Perhaps the differences lies in being the opposite-sex parent. Mothers have a soft spot for sons. But the same is probably true for fathers and daughters. Only fathers are accused of being wrapped around a daughter's finger. "Daddy's girl" and "Mama's boy" are revelatory depictions of parent-child relationships that do not easily translate to the opposite gender. "Daddy's boy" does not connect to our imagery; neither does "Mama's girl."

While mothers are raising daughters, they set in motion a relationship bond that can be stronger than a three-strand cord and as complex as the latest television serial drama.

The relationship between mothers and daughters is both mystical and magical, both connecting and confounding. As women we share a range of emotions and experiences that teach girls to become women. Mother watches daughter grow, and tries to guide her through life phases with a gentle touch. Sometimes mother watches tearfully as she allows her female progeny space to make mistakes, suffer heartbreak or betrayal, experience victory, and endure defeat.

Mothers and daughters experience a great many intimate experiences in a lifetime. These bonding times can begin with shopping trips to find the perfect outfit with shoes and hair accessories to match. There are the everyday times as a daughter sits between her mother's knees, getting her hair combed or pressed. Mother may be playing her favorite music or talking on the phone sharing a bit of hot gossip with her best friend. While daughter sits in silence and listens, mother brushes and combs, pulls, twists, and curls.

As daughter grows up, she learns things only mother can teach: how to sit with her legs together, how to speak in ladylike tones, the intricacies of feminine hygiene, and the importance of having a good girlfriend. Daughter leaves home knowing that a woman gets her hair done and keeps her nails and makeup looking good. Her wardrobe is respectable. She leaves home knowing how and why to rub Vaseline on ashy elbows and knees and she has the proper attire for the proper occasions.

Mother tearfully packs up daughter as she leaves home to attend college. In the suitcase are mother's hopes and dreams for daughter. First, that she will obtain a good education, one that will prepare her to take care of herself for life. The other desire packed along is the hope that daughter will find a suitable mate for life. If both happen, there is rejoicing. If only one happens, mother can still be proud of daughter's accomplishments.

Mother is there as daughter accesses her feminine rites of passage—her first trip to the beauty parlor, her first date, not being told to leave the room when the conversation shifts, establishing a household of her own, planning her wedding and getting married, having children.

Those are such significant and impactful times. They are indeed rites of passage. When daughter is given permission to pick out her own dress and shoes, she has made another transition. When mother and aunts and grandmothers begin to discuss topics and daughter is allowed to remain in the room, she has reached an important milestone.

Included in those rites are both joy and sorrow. After the first love can come the first heartbreak. After establishing the household come the sacrifices that must be made to be able to pay the bills. After the wedding come the realities of give-and-take in marriage. Mother is there to share in the reality with a few stories that encourage daughter to hang in there.

Daughter's rites of passage include mother—who has much more experience in human relations—speaking to daughter in woman-to-woman language about marriage, about motherhood, about life.

The woman-to-woman connections between mothers and daughters last a lifetime and extend beyond blood. Because as we grow up and have children of our own, we learn that we never grow too old to benefit from the maternal love that springs from an older woman's heart. She may be the woman who encourages you as you struggle in your high-powered job and try to fulfill your duties as a wife and mother. She may be the church mother who takes you back to your early days of growing up in church.

As we mother younger generations, we are still mothered into the newest challenges life poses. When the angel of the Lord visited Mary in Luke 1, immediately thereafter she paid a visit to her older relative, Elizabeth. Even as Mary approached her, Elizabeth had words of affirmation and encouragement for her. Perhaps Mary's own mother had passed away, or maybe she simply wanted the consolation of a mother figure who could empathize with her. After all, both had experienced a miraculous move of God. And since Elizabeth had been walking with the Lord for a much longer time, she could offer comfort to her young relative.

Elizabeth helped Mary to understand the magnitude of her gift. As young women we often devalue or dismiss our worth. Youthful insecurities may tempt us to compromise ourselves because we want to be liked or loved or appreciated or affirmed. The older, maternal figures in our lives help us to put our gifts into proper perspective and assign them value. Whether we devalue ourselves in relationships, on the job, or in our friendships, our maternal sisters help us to uncloud our vision and see our own true worth.

The wisdom from which we drink may come from a birth mother, an adoptive mother, or a "play" mother, but the benefits of having a mother/sister stay with us throughout our lives. And as our souls are quenched by their libations of insight, we are then called to share them with the young women who are behind us—our daughters, granddaughters, nieces, cousins, and "play" daughters.

In sharing from generation to generation, our roots grow deeper and the branches that hold the shade leaves grow broader and give protective shelter as we grow.

Some of the greatest joys and most memorable moments in my life as a woman were being the daughter of a very wonderful woman. She surrounded me with many other mother-daughter teams, as we learned to live and love and manage life. Many of us joined various civic organizations together, walking into the room as mothers and daughters.

One of my favorite daughter memories is of the time when I was a bride—the nights and days just before and after the wedding. The entire process—the rehearsal dinner in the home where I was raised, the thank-you notes my mother had already written and stamped to mail to all our guests as we returned from our honeymoon. (It was a huge wedding, with more than twenty-five hundred guests.)

After the wedding, we shared the values and pride of my being a Johnson daughter, and now a Johnson-Cook woman who was becoming a wife. All of it was a big deal for my mom, her only daughter getting married. Even though I was the bride, it was *her* wedding. My older sibling, a brother, had married early, so she had been waiting for this moment with her only daughter.

What joy filled my soul! And best of all, there was a letter from my mother to me, to wish me happiness and pledge her love forever.

I'd moved back home the week before the wedding, because in families from the South, living together as an unmarried couple (or "shacking up," as they called it) was not an option. My fiancé moved into the apartment that would be our marital residence, while I moved back into my mother's home, where I grew up, from junior high school through high school, college, and graduate school.

There was one doorman, Carlos, who had seen me through all those transitions. But no one knew me better than my mom. I remember the night well. All of our pets had made a circle around me and slept at the foot of my bed. Then my mom came in with a letter to her daughter, a letter *for* her daughter. I tear up even today just thinking about it. Precious.

My next favorite daughter memory is when I became a mother. To have my mother standing over me was unforgettable. Another letter, for another season of life. This was likened to no other moment. She had been there with me and for me, through nine months of morning sickness, and cravings for watermelon and Häagen-Dazs butter pecan ice cream in the middle of winter storms. Yet she'd go in search of it, and like a warrior, she'd come back with treasure.

Her daughter was becoming a mother, too. Three generations were there together. Her baby was holding *her* baby. The appreciation I had for all the life lessons my mother had taught me—the discipline, the support, the sleepovers—all hit home. I suddenly realized that my mother was a living example, a living "letter" of how she felt about me, unfolding the love and strength she had for me.

In this section, mothers write letters to their daughters, letters that will be with them forever—love letters, life letters. For some, maybe, there are words they've always wanted to say, or maybe there are words they are repeating, to have an indelible place in their hearts, their lives, and their spirits.

Read with your eyes and heart, and listen with your spirit, as mothers share with their daughters letters of hope, letters of strength, letters of encouragement, letters of things they wanted to say but didn't know how or the timing wasn't right. Or the timing was right to write this particular letter, and like me, their daughter will treasure it.

Play Mothers, Daughters, and Sisters

Some cultures have a tendency to develop familial-type bonds that are based on neither blood nor marriage. The anthropological term for these relationships is *fictive kinship*. In many subcultures within the Black community we extend our familial connections beyond blood and claim mothers, grandmothers, aunts, sisters, and cousins as our "play" relatives. Even though we use such a frivolous word to describe the connection, the bond it signifies is anything but.

These bonds can be established in a variety of ways. An older woman in an apartment building may develop a maternal connection with a young mother in the next unit. The daughters of two best friends may grow up like sisters and maintain a sisterly bond throughout their lifetime. Young women may join a sorority in college or afterward, and grow to refer to other members as sisters. Those who helped to initiate a woman into the sorority may be respectfully regarded as big sisters throughout her lifetime. A young woman who does not have a close relationship with her biological mother may form a mother-daughter bond with an older spiritual woman at church.

The bond may be for a season of life, or it may last a lifetime. Our strong bonds are like the connection between Naomi and Ruth. Technically, the elder woman was the younger's mother-in-law. But once Naomi's son, Ruth's husband, had died, their relationship did not have to continue. Ruth was free to walk away from Naomi and pursue new opportunities to find a husband and start a family.

Their relationship did not end; rather, their bond became stronger. Naomi became Ruth's play mama, and by reciprocity, Ruth became a play daughter. In fairness, Naomi exhibited maternal concern for both of her deceased sons' wives. She told them to go back to their homeland and find husbands and have babies. Her urging was rooted in her love for them both. Surely Naomi didn't want to be alone, but out of love she put their interests above her own.

Whether she really wanted them to go or not, Naomi encouraged the two younger women to return to the land of their mothers, because in the Far East, mothers were responsible for the welfare of their daughters. Naomi even issued a Hebrew blessing to her daughters-in-law: "May the Lord show kindness to you, as you have shown to your dead and to me. May the Lord grant that each of you will find rest in the home of another husband" (Ruth 1:8–9, NIV).

Orpah wisely followed the sage advice of her mother-in-law. And why wouldn't she? Naomi's advice was sound and practical for such a young woman. In Orpah's defense, the situation did not look good for the three widowed women, one of whom was older. "Naomi's right," she must have thought. "I would be better off at home with my family. I don't need to go to some foreign land where they may mistreat me because I'm from a pagan nation."

Going back to her family was a safe prospect for a young woman. In the days of Orpah, Ruth, and Naomi, marriage was security. Orpah wasn't so much choosing against her in-laws as she was choosing in favor of what she perceived to be a secure future.

Instead of running back to her homeland, Ruth chose to form an even closer bond with Naomi. Perhaps she was able to take such a bold step because she knew she had nothing to lose. Maybe things were not so rosy at the home of Ruth's biological mother.

Certainly, Ruth was committed to Naomi, but she also was sufficiently invested in Naomi's God that she pronounced an oath upon herself: "May the Lord deal with me, be it ever so severely, if anything but death separates you and me" (Ruth 1:17, NIV). She recognized Israel's God as the sovereign ruler of the universe.

In the King James version of Ruth 1:14, she "clave" to Naomi, and in the New International version she "clung." It is the same word used in Genesis 2:24 when God said a man should "cleave" (KJV) or unite to his wife. As Orpah kissed her mother-in-law good-bye, Ruth reinforced her commitment to Naomi. Their bond was as close as any could be between two human beings.

Through her faithfulness to Naomi and her uncompromised acceptance of Israel's God, Ruth was blessed to marry her kinsman-redeemer. The two women bonded and benefited each other. Ruth benefited from Naomi's wisdom about how to attract Boaz's attention. Then, after Ruth and Boaz married, Naomi was able to experience the maternal love of a grandmother through her play daughter.

Whether they are acknowledged as play kin or not, women form strong sister-mother or sister-sister and sister-daughter relationships, bonds that are often stronger than any blood connection. These relationships can encourage us to take calculated risks and faith steps. The bond may fashion into that of prayer partners who lift each other up during difficult times. The fictive kin is the woman who consoles us through loss or heartbreak.

Like Ruth, our fictive or play kin can determine to stick with us with a bond so strong it lasts a lifetime. And like Naomi, through the strength of that bond formed over time, we share in each other's benefits, blessings, and bounty.

Your Habits Will Determine Your Future

DEBRA GAUSE

Don't let anyone make fun of you, just because you are young. Set an example for other followers by what you say and do, as well as by your love, faith, and purity.

I TIMOTHY 4:12, CEV

 If you want to distance yourself from the masses and enjoy a unique lifestyle, understand this: Your habits will determine your future. Negative habits breed negative consequences; positive habits create positive rewards.

It takes focus, action, personal discipline, and lots of energy—every day—to make things happen. Too many people live for immediate gratification. Please don't be one of those who live for the moment with no thought given to the future.

Here are a few questions you should ask yourself:

1. Do I need to change my lifestyle?
2. How much education do I need in order to be successful?
3. What can I offer to help someone else?
4. How can I change the world for the better?

Try not to let distractions take you away from reaching your goals. Be the best person you can be. Self-trust enables you to make clear and conscious choices. Trusting, honoring, and loving yourself means recognizing that you have a right to be happy.

Stand up and take charge of your life.

Always remember that a person who has lived well, laughed often, and loved God will leave the world better than they found it. Never lack appreciation. You are my she-ro and that's my gift to you.

My Daughter, Your Life Is Calling

DONNA WHITE

Do not be anxious about anything, but in every situation,
by prayer and petition, with thanksgiving, present your
requests to God.

PHILIPPIANS 4:6, NIV

A letter to my daughter as she anxiously awaits her college acceptance to (or rejection therefrom) TP (That Place).

My darling,

    I was all set to quote Langston's well-known line of poetry, "life for me ain't been no crystal stair," and tell you how hard my life has been. But I won't, since the title of the poem is "Mother to Son," and you are a young lady. Plus, my life has actually been kind of a hoot—no tacks, no splinters, and no boards torn up. I've had it pretty good so far, and so have you.

    But now, you want desperately want to go to TP. You want it more than you have ever wanted anything in the world. TP was made for you, and you were made for it. But if you don't get in, you say you will be miserable, because you put so much of yourself into wanting it. I *know* all about that wanting. I really do.

    So, please know this: There will be many things in your life that you will want more than life itself. Sadly, there will be times when you will not get those things. You will love a man who does not love you back, or who cannot love you right. You will fall in love with a grad school and not get in, or with a job that turns you down. You will desperately love a house that the landlord rents to another. You will love a country that erupts in flames and closes its borders just before you get there.

You will love, love, love, and lose, lose, lose. You will fall down, get up, love, and lose again. For that is the nature of life, and of love. We love. We lose. And we live to love again.

But you, my dear, are magnificent, and you will be fine. I know this deep in my heart because the one thing I wanted most in life, but almost lost, was you. And here you are.

You know your story of the three weeks you spent in the incubator, with tubes and wires keeping you alive. You've also heard how Grandma, Dad, and I held you, touched you, rocked you, and sang to you. I sang every song I ever knew, and then made up more. I've shared with you how I pleaded with God not to take you, and promised Him that I would baptize you quick if He let you live. Then, I prayed to Grandpa in heaven to watch out for you on earth.

You know the rest. That the scar across your belly is your warrior's badge, how I tickle you there when you let me, and why I hug you so tightly when you don't.

Why I can't watch medical shows, why I will not drive on the highway. Why I'm deathly afraid of snakes, of heights, of drowning, and of fire.

I can't wait for you to start your own life, yet I can't imagine mine without you. I love you so much I'm afraid to let you go. But with love comes loss, so I let you go away from me—again and again and again.

So know this much: Whether or not you get into TP is a small thing. Your life is calling, and that is a *big* thing. A big thing, indeed.

"I am so grateful that you have come. I will pour out everything inside me so that you may leave this table satisfied and fortified. Blessings on your eyes. Blessings on your children. Blessings on the ground beneath you. My heart is a ladle of sweet water, brimming over."

From The Red Tent *(St. Martin's Press, 1997), by Anita Diamant*

Legacy Lessons That Last

DR. NATALIE A. FRANCISCO

Teach your children right from wrong, and when they
are grown they will still do right.

PROVERBS 22:6, CEV

Some would say that the eldest child has the
most pressure because of being the first—the
first to be born, the first to learn the ways and
wonders of being an only child, the first to receive discipline, the first to date, and so on.

The eldest of my three daughters rose to the
challenge of being the first to receive our lessons of life. She also stepped up to the plate to
be a wonderful example to her sisters, who still willingly follow her
today while embracing their own unique giftedness and individuality.

Although I cannot exhaust everything I've said and done in my
parenting as a proud African American woman, there are six legacy
lessons that were instilled in my daughters that I desire to pass on to
other women as well.

1. Love God. Church attendance is a good start, but it's not enough.
Those we mentor must see us enthusiastically serving God with prayer,
Bible study, and service to others so that they'll desire to do the same.
Even if they stray, they'll come back to what they've been taught.

2. Fear God. Fear in this sense is defined as moral reverence. When we teach children to reverence and respect God because it is right or righteous, it becomes easier for them to respect their parents, teachers, and other authority figures.

3. Have fun, be happy, and help others. Uptight, stressed-out, selfish parents will produce uptight, stressed-out, selfish children! Life is not merely about us, but about those who are influenced and blessed· by and through us. However, we cannot help others if we are not happy, healthy, and whole ourselves.

4. Have a strong work ethic. Once a child begins to walk, she can be taught to become responsible. Chores should be given that are age appropriate and rewarded, while other responsibilities should be given to show that it is better to give of one's time, talents, and treasures than it is to receive.

5. Love learning. From infancy to the various stages of their adulthood, I've played with my daughters, taught them new things, listened to them, gotten to know them and their friends, spent quality time with them, shared personal stories, trusted them, and most important, loved them unconditionally and lavishly. Having a love for learning and instilling the same in them during each stage of their development has ensured that my daughters thrive and not just survive.

6. Learn from mistakes. By doing so, those we mentor may avoid the pitfalls we have encountered. We shouldn't live in the past, but we should learn from it so that our present and our children's future are not held captive by it.

Mentoring our daughters is critical if they are to inherit a spiritual legacy and serve as leaders in their own right. We must think generationally and realize that we must prepare our daughters to take our place in positions of leadership and influence in every arena in society as well as in global markets.

Although it is necessary for us to focus on our career paths and issues that are important to us, let us not forget to spend the necessary time and energy ensuring that the health and well-being of the family is a priority that, for the sake of generations to come, will not be compromised.

Walk in Confidence and Command Dignity and Respect

DR. THELMA DAY

> I know, Lord, that we humans are not in
> control of our own lives.
>
> JEREMIAH 10:23, CEV

 As a child growing up in the South, I was very fortunate to reap the benefits of a "parental village." I was surrounded by Christian women who spoke with authority, but who always uttered words of encouragement. My neighbor, Sunday school teacher, school custodian, music teacher, aunts, mother, and grandmother were all a part of my parental village. Each encounter with these women underscored the principles of strength, courage, wisdom, dignity, integrity, and respect.

Throughout my life, these principles have guided, nurtured, protected, provided, motivated, and helped me successfully tackle the many challenges that I have faced. My parental village showered me with prayers, love, and support. The women in the parental village taught me social graces and instilled in me the importance of self-respect and self-confidence. Moreover, they insisted that I always exhibit ladylike manners.

I will never forget my mother's chastisement after I had screamed loudly as I walked to the neighborhood grocery store. She looked me in the eyes and said, "You were screaming so loudly, I heard you inside the house! That is not ladylike and you must never do it again. Do you understand?"

For a moment, I stared at her in disbelief. I daresay I did think that she had lost her mind. While I did acknowledge that I understood, it wasn't until my freshman year in college that what she said made sense. My college classmates and I were at a party one night and a young lady began screaming and laughing so loudly that everyone around her stopped and gave her an angry stare. At that moment, I knew what my mother had meant.

This is just one of many lessons in life that transformed me to walk in confidence and command dignity and respect. More important, it confirmed that my influences were gleaned from my family's morals and values and not from society. My parental village gave flight to my dreams and aspirations and challenged me to pass invaluable lessons in life to our daughters.

Today's societal guidelines have replaced my parental village's family morals and principles. Social media, entertainers, and celebrities have written the script that has been repeatedly rolled out in the minds, hearts, and souls of our daughters. That script has stripped our daughters of self-esteem, self-confidence, and self-respect. It has encouraged them to live by chance and not by faith. Our daughters have been robbed of their understanding of the true purpose of life and the need to do unto others as they would like others to do unto them.

Sadly, their commitment to humanity is not justice, equality, and self-empowerment. Instead, it is self-destruction and a lack of self-respect and accomplishment. Unfortunately, our daughters lack the capacity to tap into the unbelievable power that emanates from faith, love, and self-worth. Our daughters' lives are challenged by drug abuse, crime, violence, sexuality, and poverty. Their lives are afflicted by an identity crisis; a sense of hopelessness, confusion, and ambigu-

WALK IN CONFIDENCE AND COMMAND DIGNITY ✲ 39

ity concerning moral values; and the negative impact of social media and competitiveness in education.

My parting words for our daughters are: Keep your mind open to all possibilities. Eliminate selfishness, envy, and jealousy from your thoughts. Live in the power of your own authority and declare that you will always exercise integrity and treat everyone with dignity and respect. Never lose sight of the magnitude of your self-worth. Wear a smile in the face of adversity. Know that the magic of faith, the power of perseverance, and the depth of determination will help you to make a way when life itself seems hopeless.

Our Children Will Fulfill Their Destiny

REV. DR. JOAN L. WHARTON

And when you welcome one of these children because of me, you welcome me. It will be terrible for people who cause even one of my little followers to sin. Those people would be better off thrown into the deepest part of the ocean with a heavy stone tied around their necks!

MATTHEW 18.5–6, CEV

GOD, we come before you supplicating, lamenting, and praying over our children, who have and will make a great mark in society. They are your children of destiny and our children of the future.

GOD of PEACE and GOD of GLORY, we come before you on behalf of a generation of children who are living in a society that does not respect their vision, mission, charge, and gift of growing, developing, and becoming men and women of integrity—but because of who their rearing, training, and nurturing comes from, they will succeed anyhow.

GOD, we come on behalf of a generation of children who are on the rise in a society that will not respect their values, goals, and worth—but because of who they are and whose they are, they will succeed anyhow.

GOD, we come on behalf of a generation of children who will speak peace to other children who are confused; give hope to other children who live in a hopeless state; exercise faith to children who live in fear; show love to a multitude of children who have no home, no parents, and no stability; and spread joy to other children who wake up every day to hunger, war, and disease but will be delivered and set free.

FATHER, we break every generation's curse and collective family captivity over the lives of our children, in the name of Jesus.

LORD, every door or gate that the enemy will try to close against our children's destiny, open it now to success and breakthroughs, in the name of Jesus.

GOD, pour out your spirit on our children. They are your sons and daughters and they will become leaders, teachers, preachers, organizers, and heads of government and nations because they will stand in spite of and because of.

BREATH OF GOD, breathe on our children, and fill them with life anew so that they may love like thou has loved and do what thou would do. In the name of Jesus I pray. Amen.

Raise the Standards

LYNN SPIVEY

> If you obey God, you will have something to leave your grandchildren. If you don't obey God, those who live right will get what you leave.
>
> PROVERBS 13:22, CEV

> One generation plants the trees, and another gets the shade.
>
> CHINESE PROVERB

What are standards? The dictionary defines standards as values, morals, ethics, principles, ideals, requirements, guidelines, norms, ranks, degrees, flags, banners, ensigns, colors, or pennants. The point I am making is that this one word, *standards*, means a lot.

I would like us to agree on the definition as "a set of values" that we as a human race should follow. However, let's look at how the military defines "raising the standards."

In order for a unit to be recognized by an officer, it has to raise its flag, or in other words, raise its standards. Today I challenge my daughters to be recognized and raise their standards.

I am in the tree planting business. Raising the standards is not about what I get out of life; rather, it's about what I give. Every day, I plant seeds, and they may not always fall on fertile ground. But the remarkable thing about nature is that the wind blows, and when you have faith and know that you are doing a thing for the right reasons, trees will grow.

Over the years, I've had the pleasure of creating a board game and app called I Got P.O.W.E.R. (Purpose, Opportunity, Wisdom, Encouragement, Resilience), which teaches people about African American history. I know God is working on me to expand it to other areas. However, I had an opportunity to see my daughter at age fifteen create a puzzle book from the game. When you think your children are not watching, they are.

We have a tendency to tell people they can be great, but we are not teaching them what they need in order to be great. Here are a few guidelines that you can follow to lead you on your way.

- **Spiritual foundation:** Know and believe there is a higher being.
- **Purpose:** Find yours and walk in it.
- **Service:** Serve your community as a volunteer for a nonprofit or other organization.
- **Lifelong learning:** Learn something new every day (read, search the Internet, talk to someone from another culture, and so forth).
- **Information sharing:** Every day you should seek to share information with someone.
- **Partnering:** Connect with someone whose goal is to raise the standards, and then each of you hold each other accountable.
- **Mentoring:** Help someone else grow: a child or another adult who may need some guidance. We all need mentors.
- **Traveling:** If you cannot afford to go out of the country, then visit another state.

Today, my daughter, is the time to raise the standards, because we are having some heat waves and need to get in the shade.

Soul Sisters: Shared Prayers and Cares

PAMELA PALANQUE-NORTH

Children are a gift from the Lord; they are a reward from Him.
PSALM 127:3, NLT

Dear Blaine and Maegan,

You are my gifts from God and I thank the Lord for this blessing every day. I leave you a legacy of:

- Spiritual strength and endurance
- Love of God, which is another way to fully love and embrace yourself and others
- A deep commitment to fairness and equality, which you should hold as a guiding principle for interacting with people, communities, and institutions
- The ability to have an enduring love for our family and friends during the best and worst of times

It has been my prayer that you continue to cultivate your passion for learning and professionalism in all that you undertake. Remember among the truly priceless items that exist in this world are the knowledge you will acquire from many sources and the integrity of your name.

My hope is that I have mirrored for you the love and happiness that I have found in my soul mate, your dad and my husband, and that you both find and grow into this type of love with your own soul mate. For this precious relationship will carry you through so many of life's challenges and joys.

I pray that you know the joy of motherhood through the child or children you bring into this world or by mothering a child that another woman has been blessed to have but cannot care for.

Please remember to always find a way to grant *grace* to those who offend, hurt, and even harm you, for this will build your character and strength in ways that you cannot imagine.

In closing, I want you to remember to "walk into" your fears, for there is great benefit to be gained and learning derived when we have overcome our fears and trials.

Always remember the women whose shoulders you now stand on, such as Francis Campos, Elizabeth Christmas, Ola Clark, Lillie Mae Washington, and Edith Diggs. They have brought you here to advance all that they struggled for and to succeed in our education, prosperity, health, and happiness.

With deep love and pride,
Your mom

Just Be You

JETOLA ANDERSON-BLAIR

Always let Him lead you,
and He will clear the road
for you to follow.

PROVERBS 3:6, CEV

Dear daughters,

Above all, you must keep God first in all that you do and in all your deliberations and decisions. Have a plan, because the absence of a plan is a recipe for failure. However, it is critical that your good plans are really God's plans. Sometimes God will take you on a path that's very different than you imagined. You must learn the art of going with the flow. Sometimes you will wrestle with God's plan and detour on your own way, only to end up back where He was leading you all along.

Choose your friends and inner circle carefully. Know that not everyone who smiles with you is smiling for you, and not everyone wants the best for you. There will be people in your life who will love you no matter what and protect your back fiercely. There also will be those who only "love" you when it's convenient or beneficial for them. You must learn to tell the difference and be prepared to be disappointed when you see whose hand is on the knife that is in your back. But learn to keep moving forward anyway.

Never compromise your integrity or lower your standards for the sake of fitting in or currying favor with others. You are God's wonderful original work of art and He made you fearfully and wonderfully (see Psalm 139:14).

Accept who you are and live your life authentically, honestly, and unapologetically. Teach others how to treat you by treating yourself with respect and exhibiting proper decorum in all settings. Don't compare yourself with others. There will always be someone who is more than or less than you in some regard.

Just be you. Don't turn down your light or small up yourself for the comfort of others. I repeat: Just be you.

Pursue a good education because it will open up doors that otherwise might be locked. Stay focused on your priority and do not allow distractions to derail you from your goal. You might think you can't afford college, but thousands of scholarship dollars go unclaimed each year. Put in the work to find the funds. It's worth it because no one will ever be able to take your education from you.

Speak kind words to others and always remember that you don't have to verbalize every thought that crosses your mind. Don't tell everything you know, and if your words won't uplift and encourage, don't say them. Compliment others liberally and celebrate others' success. Sometimes being a cheerleader feels just as good as being on the field. When people leave your presence, they should feel better than when they entered it.

When you leave the house, look like you made an effort to make yourself presentable, but never look like you tried too hard. In this regard, it's important to know the difference between style and fashion.

Don't follow trends just because everybody else is doing it. Create and cultivate your own sense of style and be confident in your personal presentation. Always choose quality over quantity and buy the best that you can afford. Know that neither price nor label is the true measure of quality. Treat the mirror as a trusted friend; it will always tell you the truth.

In matters of love, choose the one with the kindest heart. Don't fall for the big flash and splash or the sweetest rap. Go for the one who will honor, respect, and treasure you, and treat you like the queen that you are. When you make mistakes, apologize. Then forgive yourself, pick yourself up, and keep on moving. Don't half-step in anything. Give your all. Be passionate and enthusiastic and smile even when you feel like crying. I'll say it one last time: Just be you.

FAITH

Reflections ❧ *Sister Faith*

Faith and Intention
DR. RAMONA HOAGE EDELIN

This Sister Speaks About Faith!
MICHELE WILLIAMS

This Far by Faith
DR. ANNA P. SHANKLIN

More Than Just Surviving
RUTH TRAVIS

Faith as a Lifeline
CHERÉ BROWN

A Long Walk to Spelman
CAMILLE M. HENDERSON

Rejoice! God's Got This!
DR. MARJORIE DUNCAN REED

God Will Not Allow You to Lack
AYANNA MISHOE-BROOKER

Reflections *of* Sister Faith

My myriad experiences and vocational niches—pastor, police department chaplain, motivational speaker, preacher, and author—have given me an opportunity to view the complexities of women's faith in action. Most notably, I was impressed by the faith of women who have achieved neither fortune nor fame, yet possessed the ability to stand strong in the midst of trying circumstances, to walk steady during their own circumstances, and to encourage others in the face of their trials.

My encounters with such women began in my early church experiences, and indeed in my own home. As a child I was born into a family of faith and knew there was something special about my mom, my family, and the churchwomen who surrounded her, known as the "inner circle." All thirteen would later stand with her at the altar on my christening day and become my godmothers at Rendall Memorial Presbyterian Church.

My exposure to them served as my introduction to how adult females operate within their belief system—as wives, mothers, grandmothers, sisters, aunts, club members, neighbors, teachers, and friends.

As I became a young adult, I saw the faith of my mother and my father in action, though I did not understand it as such at the time. Their sacrificial investment in my brother and me was rooted in faith. They saw through the eyes of faith what could not have been seen in our temporal circumstances. An international ambassadorship was never within the vision of a young Black girl from a working family in Harlem in the 1970s. But my mother and father saw it by faith as they invested in my private school education.

When I became a woman in my own right, wearing the hats of wife, mother, pastor, chaplain, and community activist, I became even more impressed with my mother's faith. It was through her and women like her that I came to understand that when we sing "We've Come This Far by Faith," that title is more than mere words. When I hear the song I am reminded of how women have truly leaned on the Lord at every turn.

One of the greatest demonstrations of a woman's faith came to me during a conversation with my mother in the emergency room while we were waiting for her room assignment. I was scheduled to leave the next day and accompany Bishop T. D. Jakes on a speaking tour called "God's Leading Ladies." It was a significant opportunity for me to gain exposure in my ministry. As excited as I was at the prospect of speaking before thousands of women, I was torn.

My mother was terminally ill and I absolutely did not want to leave her side. Perhaps there was some part of her that didn't want me to leave either, but by faith she knew that I had another calling to fulfill. She refused to put herself in the way of God's calling on my life. Dorothy Johnson was a powerful woman of God who understood that I was born to serve Him in a capacity beyond being her daughter.

When I shared my reluctance to leave, my mom mustered the tiny bit of strength she had to tell me, "You've been prepared [by God] for this moment. You go, and you wear that designer [St. John] suit, and let God use you to bless the world."

In those two dozen or so words, my mother had given me the blessing and release that is so important for any child to have from a parent. I believe there is special significance in a daughter receiving such a blessing from her mother, and a distinct benefit to a son hearing such words from a father as well. Standing at the entryway of her transition into eternity, my mother bravely uttered, "Go."

That day she gave me the blessing to pursue my destiny without guilt. She had been with the Lord long enough to know that God would take care of her and would take care of me also. In the years since her passing, I have never forgotten that powerful demonstration of her faith.

My mother had worked as a schoolteacher, while I explored several vocational opportunities under the umbrella of ministry. She had rendered faithful service at a single church for decades, while I would serve at several congregations. Our lives had taken different paths, but she gave me the blessing and totally supported me to be the woman God had shaped me to become. By faith she pushed her baby girl eaglet from the nest so I could spread my wings and fly. And by faith she knew that God would not let me fall.

Yes, my mother and I were different in many ways, but we shared many connecting experiences. Our commonalities—as wives, as mothers, as working women, as churchwomen—remind me of how our faith has sustained us from generation to generation. I thought about how the lessons of faith pass from mother to child when I sat for the first time in the presence of my mother and my newborn child. It was a powerful moment for me.

When I consider the busy roles of the women in my mother's generation, as well as those in my own, I am reminded that we have always been multitaskers. Even from biblical times, women have taken on many roles.

In Judges 4, we are told that Deborah was a judge, a wife, and a mother. Israel's only female judge held court underneath a tree known as the Palm of Deborah. By establishing herself there, she was positioned equidistant between the holy centers of Ramah and Bethel, making decisions underneath the palm. She was a multidimensional woman who knew to draw from God before taking on another assignment. She listened to His voice before going into battle. She took the time to hear from God to get her answer.

Women are notorious caretakers. Most of us are guilty of taking care of others while neglecting our own very real needs. Deborah inspires me because she understood what many women have not learned thousands of years later: Every battle is not your battle. Deborah picked the battle that God told her to and not one that she thought was simply a good cause. Taking on assignments that God has not given us can leave us drained and unable to fulfill the responsibilities He has given us. Deborah is our affirmation that in seeking God's face, we gain the confirmation we need to move forward in the midst of our activity.

God has directed me to face many battles since leaving the cozy security of my family and my church. In my travels as an ambassador, I learned that God would provide faith connections for me everywhere I went around the world. I've met many women of faith, and some of the most powerful examples have come from ordinary women who were neither wealthy nor famous.

During the administration of President Bill Clinton, I served as a domestic policy analyst. Moving within the halls of government, I found the faith of the women there to be vibrant and strong. People often think of government as a collective of faithless entities; however, I was often inspired by the encouragement offered me by the women working in government.

During the extended period of my Senate confirmation to be appointed U.S. 3rd Ambassador-at-Large for International Religious Freedom, God would always have people, most often women, pop up, who would slide a slip of paper with a verse of Scripture in my hand as encouragement. They would tell me, "I'm praying for you."

Time and again, God sent sister-angels who would find some way to remind me to hold on and not become unglued as I awaited the confirmation process to move forward.

Faith Has No Face

The Bible reminds us in Hebrews 13:2 that we should be welcoming to strangers because we may be in the presence of angels unknowingly. My journey through the Senate confirmation process taught me that lesson in a great way.

There were familiar faces, sisters who encouraged and supported me, like my neighbor, but sometimes those angels were total strangers.

One of the angels who came into my faith space was a Lubavitcher Jewish woman who was on an Amtrak train trip with me. We somehow began to engage in conversation about faith as mothers. She felt her children had been born into a family in which she was supposed to be the kind of Jewish mother that she was. I, in turn, shared about my children being born into a family where I was the kind of Christian mother that I was. Not only did we have our diverse experiences— from our faith to our ethnicity to our experiences as mothers—God used her to minister to me in an amazingly unexpected way.

She was the angel I needed at the time—she poured into my faith. This woman happened to be the wife of a high-ranking Jewish rabbi who was dealing with religious freedom. She was able to help me at that moment in time in the way I needed it most. Our conversation during that four-hour train ride was a true affirmation of my faith and of God's grace.

When there is no other answer, in those moments when you just don't know what to do—in the world they call it being between a rock and a hard place. But what do you do when you have neither a rock nor a hard place? So my faith sister whom I met on an Amtrak train helped me to learn a great lesson on hearing God speak in the ministry of silence.

Some people say silence is deafening, but I believe it is ministry. Faith is learning to hear God speak in the ministry of silence. During those moments of silence, He speaks and gives us the peace that surpasses all understanding.

Faith is being open to God in whatever form He comes. God sent a Jewish woman, but He also sent me an orthodox Greek man and a white male evangelical Christian pastor who began to speak to me and help me with healing, as well as with how to play the game. And in Washington, that knowledge is essential to your survival.

God sent a white evangelical male at Sylvia's, a soul food restaurant in New York City. "I felt God saying you were the president's pick," he told me. "I felt the Lord saying yes to your confirmation and God told me to tell you to hold on."

That man became my best friend in Washington. We are so different on the outside, but what a blessing I might have missed had I not been open to whom God sent. That man didn't know me, and he certainly didn't owe me, but he became my help. He was God's instrument to be my ever-present aid in times of trouble (see Psalm 46:1).

The Lord had him in my life at those times I was too exhausted to even pray for myself. He didn't look like the faith partners I'd had before, but God used him to help me get a little farther on my journey. He helped me spiritually and in very practical ways, too. He taught me how to navigate in Washington. And because he, too, was a pastor, he could explain the moves in ways I could understand.

Opening myself up was a real faith step for me, I must admit. Through that experience with my white male evangelical friend, I try to help other people be spiritually open and not live in a box. Why does there even have to be a box?

Our faith calls for us to learn how to hear God. But He has to use other means to get our attention sometimes. God allows us to be positioned so that we have to receive the help that He sends. When we don't have the luxury of picking and choosing, we avail ourselves of what He has sent. When we're drowning, we'll hop on the raft God sent and stop waiting for the luxury cruise liner to come along serving champagne and caviar.

Faith is being open to however God moves, even when it doesn't look like what we think it should. And when we're quiet and waiting to hear . . . God speaks in those moments.

Faith and Intention

DR. RAMONA HOAGE EDELIN

He will do whatever you ask, and life will be bright. When others are disgraced, God will clear their names in answer to your prayers. Even those who are guilty will be forgiven, because you obey God.

JOB 22:28–30, CEV

Unlike in my grandparents' time—back in the day—today many adults do not stay in one job or career throughout their working lives. We may have many different occupations. I have been fortunate to have several meaningful work opportunities that were and are profoundly aligned with my passion and purpose in life. My work has been me and I have been my work.

In so many ways, our work defines us; we find a sense of fulfillment and identity in our jobs. But when an employment position ends, how do we keep purpose and financial viability connected? What is our place in society? Who are we?

It is in that gap that we learn the full meaning of faith: the gap between jobs; the gap between intention and performance; the gap between aspiration and reality; the gap between fear and confidence.

In that gap, we must sit down with ego and have a talk about surrender. We must sit down with pride and have a talk about humility.

We must sit down with front and have a talk about authenticity. We must sit down with what-we-think-other-people-will-think and have a talk about know-thyself. We must mature into the power of "thy will, not my will, be done."

One door closes and another one, a better opportunity, opens to us—better than before, and better than what we had thought we wanted. A new opportunity that would never have occurred to us presents itself. An old idea, lost in the rat race and passage of time, reemerges with such force it takes our breath away. The friend who has been there all along without our really noticing has a great partnership concept. Completely out of the blue, an offer is made that we cannot and should not refuse.

Then, in faith, listening for and hearing the quiet direction of spirit, we must discover the new path and walk it with unswerving certainty. Now is the time to muster the confidence and self-assurance that have slipped to the background; to rally the support systems that have been neglected; to awaken the queen inside us who has fallen into sleep and dormancy.

Now is the time to affirm the value of this decision and our success in bringing it into manifestation. Now is the time to take practical stock of the situation and manage it. Now is the time to become master.

God the good, the omnipotent, will not forsake us in trial! Thank you!

This Sister Speaks About Faith!

MICHELE WILLIAMS

You are tempted in the same way that everyone else is tempted.
But God can be trusted not to let you be tempted too much,
and He will show you how to escape from your temptations.

I CORINTHIANS 10:13, CEV

Lord, you made a believer out of me! How can you go into the hospital, know that six doctors have given up on your child, yet he gets released and goes home with a full recovery?

How can you go into the courtroom and win a very unusual case, in which the judge gives you forty-five minutes to tell your side of the story and hears nothing from the other side?

How can you buy a car, with no job, no one else in your family having any income, and a 300 credit score?

How can your vehicle completely shut down, in the middle of a seven-lane highway, during rush hour traffic, with cars whizzing past at forty to sixty miles per hour and you not get hit?

How can you close on a house with no down payment, or live rent-free for three years in your own home not once, but twice?

You get the gist of these situations. It is during these times when you have to know that it was God who made it so. No worries—when you are a child of God, He's got you!

These are all very real situations that have occurred, involving me and my family. It was during these times that God truly was an "eyewitness" to the circumstances, yet He was my Savior who gained the victory in each case. He allowed me to experience the extremes of these situations, yet come out of each like I had received a million-dollar check!

How can one not trust a God who will get you through and sustain you until He is ready to show you favor in your next divine blessing?

Many are not equipped to handle the heavy of whatever the situation may be. First Corinthians 10:13 (NKJV) sums it up by saying, "God is faithful . . . that you may be able to bear it."

The most difficult of all of these trials was watching my thirty-year-old son fight for his life. After leaving a restaurant with a friend, he was shot twice by an angry football fan whom he didn't even know. My son was hospitalized, in a coma and on life support for a total of forty-six days. As I slept beside him each night, too numb to pray, God took over.

His medical team did not expect him to survive after the third week. The injuries affected every organ in his body, except his heart. Four of five neighboring patients passed away—in rooms 208, 209, 210, and 218. My son was in room 211. Death was all around his room, but couldn't get in. Just trust God. Keep your faith, for He will get you through.

My son is thirty-three years old now. Remember, Jesus walked the earth thirty-three years.

This Far by Faith

DR. ANNA P. SHANKLIN

The Lord has blessed you because you believed that He will
keep His promise.

LUKE 1:45, CEV

Women face many challenges, both personally
and professionally. These trials can be of an
emotional, financial, mental, physical, and yes,
even a spiritual nature.

The question each of us must answer is not
whether we will be faced with a challenge;
rather, it is: How will we deal with the challenge when it appears? I found myself having to
deal with a challenging health issue, the death of a loved one, an intense character attack, and facing the fact that relationships I once
thought were solid were crumbling before my eyes.

I stood in a painfully difficult place. It was at this point that I realized two things. First, I had heart issues; and second, I was still
standing. How? As I thought of the heart issues, I thought of an im-
planted heart defibrillator. This device sends electrical impulses, often
undetected, to the heart anytime it identifies irregular rhythms in the
heartbeat to ensure a continued natural rhythm.

I realized I was still standing despite my challenges because of my
internal spiritual defibrillator—faith. The substance of things hoped

for and the evidence of unseen things show what God says about the story even when the page is blank.

During the annunciation visit, Elizabeth speaks to Mary the key to fulfillment of the promise. In Luke 1:45 (KJV), we find a sister speaking to another sister about faith. Elizabeth says, "Blessed is she that believed." The word believed is derived from the Greek root word for "faith" (πίστις). So, simply put, Elizabeth says to Mary, "Sister, you have come this far by faith."

Before Mary was ready to conceive, she believed. She not only conceived because she believed, but she received because she believed. This is important because not everything that is conceived results in an actual delivery. Mary's yielding her vessel in faith in Luke 1 produces results in the very next chapter, when she delivers her firstborn son (Luke 2:7).

Soul sisters, we are pregnant with possibility and we have to believe to conceive, and then receive the fulfillment of the promise that has been spoken in our lives. Soul sisters, we've got to have faith!

No matter what challenge you face, remember whose you are and who you are, and stand on the promises of God in faith. I know you get tired sometimes and circumstances seem overwhelming, but I want to let you know that you have an internal spiritual defibrillator called faith, just like the defibrillator that provides lifesaving shocks to the heart.

Faith says, "I believe my life's purpose is greater than my pain, so I can't give up now."

In the natural world, external defibrillators emit a *boop* sound as the shock is administered. So I charge you, my sister, even in the midst of your challenges, to activate your internal, spiritual defibrillator. In due season you shall reap if you faint not. So don't faint. Activate your faith!

- When you feel like throwing in the towel, don't throw it in. *Boop!* Self-defibrillate and believe.

- When you feel like walking out the door, don't walk. *Boop!* Self-defibrillate and believe.
- When you feel like bailing out on the mission, remember the message given to you, and don't bail. *Boop!* Self-defibrillate and believe.

We've come this far by faith. We're still standing, and because of our belief our faith will see us through to the next level.

Boop! Self-defibrillate. Your destiny is calling you!

More Than Just Surviving

RUTH TRAVIS

> Jesus said to the woman, "You are now well because of your faith. May God give you peace! You are healed, and you will no longer be in pain."
>
> MARK 5:34, CEV

On Tuesday, November 27, 2007, two days before my sixty-second birthday, I heard my doctor say four words that every woman dreads: "You have breast cancer." Like the woman in the biblical text, the fear of the diagnosis caused me to feel anxious and nervous about how long I had to live.

I knew I had to get to Jesus right away! I silenced my mind in order to not be trapped by fear, my spiritual belief reflecting my approach to this life-threatening disease. I had to be my own best advocate. Between tears and prayers, I learned how to become fully reliant on God.

I started to meditate on positive words that begin with the letter *C* (*Christ, cruise, candy, cake, clothes, conqueror*). It was during this moment of silence when I heard the Lord say, "This is not sickness unto death."

I responded, "Okay, Lord, how are we getting through this?" It was very clear to me that this was not the time for a pity party. It was time to activate my faith over fear.

I needed ferocious fortitude to guide me through the unfamiliar terrain of surgery, recovery, and radiation treatment—which lasted six weeks, five days a week, twice a day. Like the woman in the text, I needed desperate faith in order to press my way forward.

The activation of my faith has enabled me not to just survive breast cancer, but also to view my life with confidence and think outside the box. I have strategically aligned myself with The Journey Continues, an African American breast cancer survivor support group that was birthed in the family room of my home.

I am not just surviving. I am working on achieving my dream to have a "Pink House" where breast cancer survivors can come for rest, relaxation, and restoration. Jesus said to the woman in the text, "Daughter, you took a risk of faith, and now you're healed and whole. Live well, live blessed! Be healed of your plague" (Luke 8, MSG).

My assignment is to spread the good news of what the Lord is still doing for me. I have made up my mind that no matter what comes my way, no matter how difficult my assignment is, I am not just a survivor; I am a conqueror.

Through faith, I am expecting God to do the extraordinary because it brings Him honor and glory. I am a prime example of just how good God is. I am surrounded by His favor and I can and will do all things through Christ who gives me the strength.

My best days are ahead of me as "the journey continues."

Faith as a Lifeline

CHERÉ BROWN

I will bless you with a future filled with hope—a future of
success, not of suffering.
JEREMIAH 29:11, CEV

 I was born with a silver spoon in my mouth
and raised in a Christian home, and both parents were pastors. I was taught the things of the
spirit early on and I accepted Christ as my personal Savior at the age of ten.

I had the opportunities to matriculate at
the finest schools of higher education, earning
a master's degree by age twenty-three, and I
married before starting a family. How could
trouble ever find me? I thought I was nestled safely in the bosom of
middle-class America. In my mind, I was grounded firmly on a foundation of faith and family.

I had no idea that life would come to shake that foundation so
hard it would almost knock the wind out of me. After five years of
marriage, my husband (who was a saved lay leader in our church) decided one morning to pack a bag and leave our family for an alternative lifestyle. I was utterly and completely shattered. I became
depressed and even was prescribed antidepressants.

I was left with our two sons, ages twelve and two, and a new home and car that I could not afford to keep up on my own. My family was supportive, but couldn't be there in the dark of night when the pain was so great that I wanted to somehow just disappear.

This kind of trouble was way over my head. This kind of pain was more than I could bear, but I remembered that I had a Father who had plans for me (Jeremiah 29:11). This happened to be the guiding Scripture for our church. My mother and pastor, the late Reverend Dr. Eleanor Bryant, had instilled this promise in me. Despite lonely, tearful nights, foreclosure, and car repossession, I decided to sort through my tears, grab my faith, and hold on tight.

My faith became my lifeline. For a while that was all I had. I woke up each day trusting that God would keep me and that He held the plan for my future. Now, as a full-time therapist and consultant, as well as a mother with two adult sons, one daughter-in-law, and one grandson, I use the strength gained from my testimony to help others.

God has empowered me to turn pain into purpose, and that is what I teach. My ministry is jam-packed with power gained through personal experience. God is able to do abundantly more than you could ever ask or think.

So know, my dear sister, that you can make it through whatever situation you find yourself in. Just take a moment to focus on your faith, grab hold tightly, and stand. God has the plan.

> *"And we know that all things work together for good to them that love God, to them who are called according to His purpose."*
>
> *(Romans 8:28, KJV)*

A Long Walk to Spelman

CAMILLE M. HENDERSON

Faith makes us sure of what we hope for and gives us proof of
what we cannot see. It was their faith that made our ancestors
pleasing to God. Because of our faith, we know that the world
was made at God's command. We also know that what can be
seen was made out of what cannot be seen.

HEBREWS 11:1–3, CEV

My earliest acts of faith were inexplicably bold.
My choices never made sense to others—they
barely made sense to me. Yet somehow I managed to succeed despite overwhelming doubt.

The formation of my faith started my junior
year of high school, when I realized that Harvard University, my top choice for undergraduate studies, was not a good match for a small-town
girl like me. I remember walking around Harvard's campus thinking,
"There is no way that I can come straight from high school to a place
this big!"

As I scrambled to find an institution suitable for my fresh-out-of-
high-school mentality that would still provide demanding academic
pursuits, Spelman College appeared on my radar. Nationally ranked
as the top historically Black college, complemented by a surplus of
supportive alumnae who were excelling in their respective fields,
Spelman quickly became my new Harvard.

But attending Spelman meant twenty-five hundred dollars in loans and no means of financial support, so my mother resisted. She feared that she wouldn't be able to pay for her child's education. At the time, I interpreted her fear as complete rejection of Spelman. Any conversation we had about college always ended in an argument. My persistence and her refusal burdened our relationship.

The risk of Spelman becoming a dream deferred was my first real test of faith. This was the first time I had to fight for what I believed in. It was the first time I realized that faith takes hold of our actions when we least expect it. I didn't know why, but I just knew I had to get to Spelman—my faith took hold of me and it wouldn't let go.

I honestly didn't realize that my faith was leading me until I was on my way to Spelman for an overnight program for admitted students. On the way there, I woke up to my grandmother in the driver's seat, her face flooded with tears, thanking God for "bringing us so far." I cried and thanked God with her—our faith in Him had made the seemingly impossible possible.

During my visit, I was introduced to the Bonner Scholars Program, which eventually awarded me a scholarship covering full tuition and a stipend for all four years of college. Because of my faith I became a Bonner Scholar, and it was in faith that I assumed larger responsibilities. I was given much; therefore, much was expected. I started to see my faith as a muscle—the more I exercised its power, the better the outcome of what was required of me.

Exercising faith pushes us to acknowledge that everything we need to live, speak, and walk boldly is already inside us. It took insurmountable obstacles, a broken relationship, and painful rejection for me to be involuntarily led by faith—all so that I might learn to exercise my faith voluntarily. Through it all, the greatest lesson I have learned is that we must allow our faith to lead us, and follow it with every bit of our might.

Rejoice! God's Got This!

DR. MARJORIE DUNCAN REED

But I will still celebrate because the Lord God saves me.

HABAKKUK 3:18, CEV

 Habakkuk? I'm going through so many things at one time and the Lord leads me to read the book of Habakkuk? Really, God? I have questions regarding what I'm going through. I'm starting to ask, "Are you still with me?" My faith is shaken, or wavering—whatever word you want to use. I'm praying, but God is not answering.

In chapters one and two, Habakkuk was complaining about the iniquity in the land and about having to wait for an answer from God regarding so many issues. He sounded like me. Trying to hold on in difficult times is not easy, especially when it feels that God has taken a sabbatical.

The enemy is attacking your family; your health is not responding to medications; your bills are past due; your strength is failing and your heart is broken. And every time you turn on the radio or the television, you talk and pray like Habakkuk: "Lord, do you see what is going on down here?"

After Habakkuk asked his questions in chapters one and two, he prayed his prayer in chapter three. He declared, "I know what I'm gonna do." Here's your answer. Don't miss it. "I'm gonna rejoice in the Lord!"

Habakkuk had looked back over the previous years and realized what great things God had done for him. He began to rejoice. I had to remind myself of God's track record. He's brought me through surgeries when others counted me out. I had to watch my best friend, who always had my back, suffer and die. Alone, but not alone. And then the Word jolted me. *Rejoice! God's got this!* He opened doors in corporate America when others tried to close them.

Marjorie, you don't think God can handle this problem? So I went to verse 19: "The Lord God is my strength, and He will make my feet like hinds' feet, and He will make me to walk upon mine high places."

I began to bless His name. I didn't need to read a faith Scripture. I just needed to be reminded of my faith in God. God can! In other words, *Rejoice! God's got this!*

God Will Not Allow You to Lack

AYANNA MISHOE-BROOKER

But you must learn to endure everything, so that you will be
completely mature and not lacking in anything.

JAMES 1:4, CEV

I had a great job working in the Wall Street
area. I was making good money! However, in
my seventh year of employment with the company, I kept hearing God clearly tell me,
"Ayanna, you are in a good season *right now*.
Pretty soon this season will end, so prepare."

Ultimately, God's warning came to pass. I
was part of a devastating major layoff. Right after I received word that
my position would be eliminated, I went for a walk and prayed: "Lord,
I'm praying for *continuity*. May my family *lack in nothing*. God, please
do not allow a break in my family's finances, health, peace, and in areas
I can't even think of."

I offered my prayer in faith, knowing that God would not fail me,
my two young children, or my husband (who was also unemployed,
but pastoring a church that was not financially able to support him as
a "full-time" pastor).

I immediately started looking for employment. With my faith,
education, and work experience, I just knew I would be reemployed
within two weeks. My thoughts were so wrong! It took exactly seven

months for employment to open up to me, and even that was only a temporary assignment. But a few weeks later, I received a full-time offer. As soon as my eleven-year-old heard the news, he said, "Mom, you taught me that the number seven means completion. You worked at the old job for seven years and you didn't have another job for seven months. You've completed your course."

He blew my mind!

My severance ran out after three months, but remember, God had prepared me to store up for the famine. I was obedient unto God like Pharaoh was to Joseph. Now, the day before I received the call for the temporary position, which began that *next* day, we only had three hundred dollars left in my bank account, with about three thousand dollars in bills facing us for the next month. The full-time employment wasn't scheduled to begin for another three to four weeks. Nonetheless, I was able to work in my temporary position until the full-time position started. That was "continuity"! On top of that, after I accepted the full-time position, my husband received an offer of employment with a company that offered non-conflicting hours with his pastorate.

With the exception of a scheduled surgery, none of my family got sick. We never went hungry or needed anything. We even went on a vacation that had already been paid in full before the layoff. Of course, several sacrifices and cutbacks had to be made, but we used wisdom.

The journey wasn't easy and the emotions were sometimes volatile, but I stayed the course, kept the faith, trusted God, remained steadfast in prayer and fasting, and continued to preach and teach God's Word.

My prayer for you is that you remain steadfast in times of uncertainty. Endure, my sister, and be patient. As always, God will come through.

LAUGHTER

Reflections ❧ *Three Simple Ingredients*

The Love of Laughter
DR. CARLISS McGHEE

Reflections ✒ Three Simple Ingredients

Love. Live. Laugh. What a simple trio of ingredients forms this proven recipe for a life well lived. When the 9/11 tragedy happened, I was on the frontlines. As an NYPD chaplain for twenty-one years, I and my colleagues were some of the first responders. There were several assignments, including helping those who had been 911 operators and others get through this horrific time. But the internal woundedness was taking its toll, and after sixty days of intense recovery and rescue efforts, I couldn't help myself. I pulled over to the side of the road and began to cry. Not just small, polite tears, but bawling. It was too much.

I found an ad in the newspaper for a comedy workshop that was being offered at Carolines on Broadway, a comedy club in New York. I took the workshop for about three weeks, and then went to the club and listened to the comics. No one had laughed in a long time.

Fear had replaced fun in my life, and my soul needed restoration. I needed to laugh. I mean I needed gut-busting, deep belly laughter. And I got it.

Laughter really is medicine for the soul, as the proverb says. It releases enzymes and endorphins into the system, physiologically changing how we operate and respond.

I hope you will read some of these devotionals and smile. More than that, maybe you'll even laugh. One of the greatest rewards is, after a long day or week, getting together with my soul sister friends, who don't mind laughing and giggling. We allow ourselves to figuratively and literally let our hair down, laughing until tears come out, because we need to. Laughter is what we've been waiting for.

Look for reasons to laugh and be happy. Be the cause for rejoicing in someone else's life. Be the laugh someone needs to break her string of sorrow. Laughter is contagious, so just by lightening up, you can help others, too. Begin by not taking yourself too seriously. Laugh at your mistakes, your imperfections. Laugh when you momentarily forget your own child's name. Chuckle when you forget it's Saturday morning and you get up and get dressed for work. Smile at your thighs and find amusement in your long, skinny fingers. Please don't rob yourself of joy because of life's demands. You will find yourself far better able to meet life's challenges when you pack up your sense of humor and take it with you everywhere you go.

Just Joy

Every so often someone crafts a song that connects with popular culture. You can hear it everywhere—on the radio, in elevators, being hummed in the streets by strangers. In the late 1980s, that song was Bobby McFerrin's "Don't Worry, Be Happy." The song used a simple tune to advocate an uncomplicated but powerful message.

Christians sometimes find it difficult to simply be happy for no reason or for every reason. Every so often we experience splashes and flashes of joy that overcome us. We look at our family watching a movie together and we're happy. We hear our elderly mother make a risqué comment and we're happy that she still has a sharp mind with a sense of humor. We see a three-year-old experience the thrill of jumping into a puddle of water or running through a lawn sprinkler.

Life presents real challenges, so every splash of joy we experience should be relished wholeheartedly.

As we get older, most of us realize that the simple joys that mean the most in life cannot be bought or coerced. They just happen, and their sheer simplicity makes them divine. Often they are moments we cannot re-create—the silliness of taking selfies with a childhood friend, a dog scratching his back in the grass, or the warmth of that first sip of freshly brewed coffee on a cold day. Because the moments cannot be reconstructed exactly as they happened before, they are snippets in time when we can praise God for the sheer joy of joy. Not joy in spite of problems, but the momentary rush of good feeling that may come as quickly as it goes; therefore, it should not be dismissed or ignored.

The Love of Laughter

DR. CARLISS McGHEE

If you are cheerful, you feel good; if you are sad, you hurt all over.
PROVERBS 17:22, CEV

I was most vulnerable to being teased while growing up. I was tall for my age, wore thick glasses, and had the most unmanageable head of hair. So, kids had very nasty and mean things to say about me 24-7. Fortunately for me, I grew up in a household that laughed often and had such a wonderful sense of humor. Both my parents gave me a safety net of laughter to defend myself against the world.

Whenever I questioned why kids didn't particularly embrace my looks, my mother would respond by saying things like, "God made you, not those folks at school or across the street, and He didn't make no junk. You got four eyes because God gave you two and the doctor gave you two more—now without those four eyes, girl, you can't see! You are tall because your daddy's tall—they need you to see over the little kids."

My family always had a way of making light of certain situations. I can remember asking my mother if I was cute, and in her motherly way, laced with her sense of humor, she would say, "Monkeys are cute.

Besides, all the cute kids I knew growing up grew out of their cuteness by the time they were ten."

I learned early on that not everyone was going to embrace God's masterpiece, me. But I learned to love me and all that came with being me. The gift of laughter has allowed me to create space for others to feel safe and loved.

Laughter has kept me grounded and so appreciative of those things around me. When you find out early in life that most things are not that serious, you open up to a world that offers you unimaginable freedom and joy.

The freedom to experience all that God has for your life, your gifts and talents, is exposed earlier and your journey in life stays in motion. Our cravings to get to our destination dissipate; we lose our insecurity and the need to be judgmental.

Laughter gives us the ability to adapt to those unfavorable situations. When circumstances are presented in life that are painful and difficult to understand, remember: We serve a good and loving God.

I am reminded of how humble and forgiving Nelson Mandela was after twenty-seven years of imprisonment. He never lost his sense of humor and he laughed often. So, try to observe someone who has gone through the storms of life and is still laughing. Laughter is not a secret; it's a decision that we make when choosing to be happy.

LIFE BALANCE

Reflections ❧ *Play as Well as Pray*

You Go, Girl!
KENYA L. MOORE (LADY K)

Spiritual Discipline Yields a Balanced Life
MARY SHEFFIELD

I Am . . .
GWEN FRANKLIN

A Soul Sister's Guide to Balancing Life with Praise and Prayer
M. GASBY BROWN

Be True to Yourself
RONNEAK M. LEE

The Big Balance Lie
DR. AVIS JONES-DeWEEVER

Showers of Blessing
EYESHA K. MARABLE

Reflections ❦ *Play as Well as Pray*

While I was in my seventh year of pastoring, I wrote *Too Blessed to Be Stressed*. I was compelled to write it because I was burned out. I'd had no female pastors in the Baptist tradition to help mentor me through handling all the demands that were pressing on me. I was a single pastor trying to manage the many ministry responsibilities. I hadn't set any boundaries in place to help me. I didn't know how to establish office hours and stick to them. I didn't know how to say no. I didn't know how to take vacations. My life was in overdrive and I didn't know how to stop.

When I needed it most, the Lord gave me an amazing gift of a sabbatical year at Harvard University. When the news got out that I was taking a yearlong leave from my church, pastor friends from around the country cautioned, "You're going to lose your church if you do this." My response to them all was, "If I don't, I'm gonna lose myself." I was at that verge and I understood it better than anyone.

At Harvard, I lived on the Business School campus, which was adjacent to the Charles River. Every morning I would walk around the waterway and reflect on Psalm 23:2–3 (NKJV): "He leads me beside the still waters. He restores my soul."

In that sabbatical year, God brought me back and gave me verbiage that I was able to share with other women to keep them from going to the place of deep weariness where I had fallen.

Many women experience episodes of burnout: when you have a

job you don't feel like going to; when you don't feel like getting out of bed; when you feel like you're living in a hole. It's not depression. It's burnout. I wrote the book to guide women to bounce back from burnout, or hopefully, to prevent it.

Walking beside those quiet waters I learned what it meant to have balance in my life. Through that experience I learned the root word of vacation means to vacate. I experienced the restoration that King David exalted as God restoring our soul. My time off helped me understand that the process of engaging in recreation (which many of us don't even deal with) means God is re-creating us.

Women give. We give to our families, nuclear and extended. We give to our jobs and our coworkers. We give to our best friends, to community groups, and even to strangers on the street. Women pour out so much that we don't always recognize when we need a refill of what we've dispensed.

We pour out to husbands, to children, to careers, to friends, to church. And those are great things, but every vessel gets empty if it continues to pour out with no replenishment. The largest economy-size container will eventually get to its bottom if nothing is ever poured back into it.

Many women don't know how to give ourselves permission to sit down and rest. Sometimes we experience feelings of awkwardness in stopping. We're so used to being busy and going and giving. We don't know what to do even if we do stop. Even years after writing *Too Blessed to Be Stressed*, I find myself still doing busy work even when I'm off—making lists, checking e-mails and voice mails, or looking up something online. It's just busy work.

Women of color sometimes don't know how to slow down. We're working twice as hard to prove that we belong in the place where we are, that we have what it takes. We're working harder to prove ourselves on the job, working harder to keep our children from getting lost in a system that seems eager to push them aside. We're ever aware of the need to try and be ahead of the game.

I remember working as a White House Fellow during the Clinton administration. I had a newborn baby, which understandably consumed a significant amount of time. I thought that getting there at seven thirty a.m. meant I was doing great. After all, I was there before eight. But some people had been there since six thirty, and before the workday officially had begun they were already caught up on all the news of the day from several sources—the *Wall Street Journal*, the *New York Times*, the *Washington Post*, etc.

Staying late wasn't always an option because I had to make some tough choices between spending time with my baby and putting in more time on the job. We have tough choices as women. We don't always have the options that men have regarding whether to invest our time in our families or our careers.

Trying to have it all, many times we can lose our way. We're living on the edge and don't know how to turn it off. We lose our sense of self. We lose our way and it impacts our lives in dramatic ways.

"Sit down and rest your nerves."

When my body feels out of sync, I know that it's time to, as the elders used to say, "Sit down and rest your nerves." Many conditions can contribute to our feeling this way: stress, menstrual cycles, anemia, hormonal changes, fatigue—and trying to keep the same level of activity going all the while. Just imagine how the hemorrhaging woman must have felt in Mark 5. She was weary and anemic from more than a decade of excessive blood loss. By now, she was not only sick and tired; she was sick and tired of *being* sick and tired.

It's important to heed the body's call to stop and rest. If we don't, our bodies will find ways to make us stop. Stress often manifests through physical illness, mental duress, or emotional volatility.

It's okay to stop. It's even essential that we stop at times and play. Give yourself permission. Find things you like to do, and do them, even if you do them alone. Be comfortable with yourself in your own skin, in your own time. As author and media psychologist Dr. Gwendolyn Goldsby Grant advises, "You're not going by yourself; you're going WITH yourself."

Whether you do it with yourself, by yourself, or with others, stop and enjoy. Laugh as much as possible. Proverbs 17:22 says that a joyful heart is like good medicine. It's true that laughter and enjoyment cause our endorphins to kick in, which makes us feel good. I laugh as much as possible. I place myself around silly people to help me laugh.

When you take rest breaks, your rhythm gets restored. Bishop T. D. Jakes talks about the human trichotomy of mind, body, and spirit. Just as we have a triune God, we also have three parts of the self, which need to be in balance for all three to flow properly. They all have equal input in our development and we must give attention to each.

For instance, everyone who knows me well knows that I do not function well after ten p.m., so I schedule my life to honor my body, which is ready for rest at that time. Occasionally I push it, but mostly, I acquiesce. I've even left trusted houseguests to fend for themselves when my body told me it was time to shut down, but the party was not over.

Respect your needs—for space, for humor, for quiet, for fellowship—and fulfill them. Honor your appointments with yourself to be alone or to go to a movie or to treat yourself to some quiet time. Just because you get an invitation doesn't mean you have to attend. You made an appointment with yourself, and that's just as important.

Until you make "me time" a habit, you may feel guilty about doing something just for you. The people around you can make it even harder because they might not buy into the you who takes care of herself. They want the you who cooks for them, drives them all over town, and loans them money whenever they ask. If you're overloaded by the needs of others, be a friend to yourself and do what is necessary to get your life back in balance.

Go Back to the Maker

Sometimes we have to live out of balance for short periods of time—going back to work after having a baby, starting a new career, working two jobs to pay down debt, working and going to school full time. We can do it for a while, but life was not meant to be lived that way. It's like a car driving on its rims when all the tires are flat. We can do it for a while, but if we don't stop, we will only incur more damage.

We hit potholes in life. When we do, we have to figure out the damage done by that pothole so we can get back on the road. A car can run for a while when something is wrong, but it can't keep going on and on like that. Your body is the same way.

When your car gets out of whack, you have to take it back to the maker. There may be many mechanics along the way, but no one knows your vehicle like the one who made it—the intricacies, what caused the problem in the first place, and the best repair method.

When your life gets out of alignment and you are not running properly, take it back to your Maker, who blessed you and made you. Our Maker knows our intricacies, every hair on our heads. God knows our makeup, what repairs we need, the accidents we've had, the damage that's been done, and the maintenance we require. Our Maker knows why we are not performing optimally. He knows the damage that can be done by the blowouts, the accidents, and the potholes. He knows how to fix and restore us so that we can do what we were created to do.

For me, restoration comes from water. I go back to the water and that's the beginning of my renewal. I call it "watching the waves dance." When I'm feeling out of sync, whatever city or country I'm in, I'll get to some water and watch the waves dance.

Why waves? I'm fascinated by them, probably because they're unattached and nonconforming. I watch the freedom with which they move and wonder, Why can't we just dance like the waves? After watching them dance for a while, I start to feel my rhythm come back. All I need is to feel a single misty drop on my skin, and it's like the waves are telling me, "It's okay, baby girl. You're coming back." When I feel myself becoming whole again, then I know that coming out on the other side I will have to do something different.

Lamentations 3:22–23 (ESV) reads:

> "The steadfast love of the Lord never ceases;
> His mercies never come to an end;
> they are new every morning;
> great is your faithfulness."

At the end of each day that God allows you to live, close the chapter. Don't wrestle. You did the best you could for that day. Then, when you wake up the next day, it's time to say, "Lord, give me this day. I'm putting aside the old. I don't want to get ahead of you. Give me what I need for this day. It is my present to be in your presence, to be one of your children."

God makes us new, says the apostle Paul in 2 Corinthians 5:17. At various points in life, God will lead us to something new, and the time will come when you have to make some changes and have some new beginnings. You do have to close some chapters before you can begin the next one.

When we accept this fact of life, we can navigate the changes more smoothly. Sometimes people find it hard to make a move, to push away. So we make excuses or find reasons to move to the next chapter. Instead of picking a fight to get away, pick a plan. It enhances balance in your life and stops you from going to the deep, dark place of burnout.

That's why I resonate with Deborah in the Bible. She understood time management. She didn't run back and forth trying to meet all the needs of her people. She met their needs, and her own, by positioning herself so the people would come to her to resolve their issues (Judges 4:5).

I had the privilege of traveling with Bishop T. D. Jakes as the motivator during a two-year, five-person God's Leading Ladies tour. As I shared my stories, the crowd would go wild when I got to the part about life balance. I compared my life before my sabbatical to a car that had hit a pothole but had kept on going.

When I used that analogy, nearly every woman could relate, whether she was the driver or the passenger, because on this highway called life, our wheels are not always rotating smoothly. Some days our tires get flat. Our spiritual "trunks" get packed too full, and the oil under our hood runs out. We get out of balance and need a holy alignment. Just as there is a triune God—Father, Son, and Holy Ghost—we must be in balance in three aspects: mind, body, and soul. For me, it means engaging in laughter, getting eight hours of sleep, and being near a body of water bordered by sand.

But if I work hard, I must balance my life and play and pray hard. Life balance is about getting one's spiritual groove back. As you're reading, think of ways to get your own life balance. Think of a seesaw in a park, and make sure you're evenly balanced.

A seesaw cannot have uneven weight. Neither can your life. You cannot live weighed down in a lopsided life. Pressure cannot mount and never be evened out.

Ask yourself what it will take to make you whole. I've recently rediscovered my love for swimming. God has it so divinely planned that the place where I live is right next door to an Olympic-size swimming pool. So I swim two or three mornings a week, not only for physical exercise but also to clear my head, meditatively starting my day. Look around you. See what, and who, surrounds you. Your answer might just be within your reach.

My answer was right next door, in an adjacent building. Yours may be just a prayer or a phone call or a friend away.

You Go, Girl!

KENYA L. MOORE (LADY K)

Christ gives me the strength to face anything.
PHILIPPIANS 4:13, CEV

Have you ever felt like you wanted to quit, stop, throw your hands up and say, "I just cannot take it anymore"? Have you ever felt like what you were pursuing was no longer worth the effort? Sometimes life can throw so many curveballs your way that it seems like you cannot catch even one. You ask yourself, "Will I ever hit a home run?"

Wow, life is sometimes just like a baseball game. Just imagine the game in which you are the batter who is up to hit the ball. Bases are loaded with potential, promise, and provision. The pitcher throws. The umpire yells, "Strike one!" Then, "Strike two!"

Oh, my gosh! You swing and hit the ball, but the umpire says, "Foul ball!"

You ask, "What in the world?" At this point in the game of life, you are frustrated and feel like quitting. You just want to stop and sit out the rest of the game.

Well, I want you to know that a foul ball does not mean it is over. It just means you get another try.

That *is* right! Oh, you thought it was time to stop? No, ma'am.

Don't stop now! You go, girl! There are too many great things in store for you that are yet ahead of you.

You already have the *courage to sustain you*. Courage will move you to do what you think you cannot do and conquer every obstacle set in your way.

You have the *confidence to keep you*. Be confident of this very thing: that He who has begun a good work in you shall perform it until the day of Jesus Christ and that the work that has been started in you shall be completed within you (see Philippians 1:6–7, NKJV).

You have the *commitment to carry you*. You have to be committed to your visions and dreams; no one can take this away from you.

You have to *change your response to create ways out of no way*. When you change how you respond to your life situations, you will change how you think and act. Let your response be "It is well."

You go, girl! I have made it through challenging situations and I know you can, too. Don't stop, because courage will sustain you, confidence will keep you, commitment will carry you, and changing your response will create ways out of no way.

You go, girl!

Spiritual Discipline Yields a Balanced Life

MARY SHEFFIELD

All of you surely know that you are God's temple and that His Spirit lives in you.

1 CORINTHIANS 3:16, CEV

If we let it, life can break us down. I know. I've been there. There've been days I felt like giving up. There were days I questioned my circumstances, emotions, and calling. I've turned to friends, to my pastor, and to others, looking for answers they couldn't give.

I remember all the trouble, fruitless relationships, and situations I found myself in when I thought I could lead my own life. Life has humbled me, literally forcing me to my knees crying out, "Lord, I want more of you, and less of me!"

I didn't get to that point until I was strategically placed where I had no one to turn to. I became desperate for God's spirit. When I look back at the times I felt like breaking, it was truly the spirit of God that kept me. The balance, comfort, and peace the spirit brings, no one or nothing on this earth could ever compete with or compare.

No matter what you're facing at this very moment, God wants

you to look within. The spirit of God will keep you from breaking, and that spirit dwells within you.

As women of destiny, we must make time for ourselves, and more important, for our spirits. True balance and happiness come from within. It's what I call bliss! Sometimes we have to hit the pause button on the demands of life, turn off reality TV, stay home on a Friday evening, and just say no, so that we can be still in the presence of God.

Over the years, I've come to realize the importance of spiritual discipline for living a peaceful and balanced life. Spiritual discipline is behavior that augments our spiritual growth and enables us to grow to spiritual maturity.

God's spirit lives within us but often we don't pay any attention to Him at all.

Spiritual discipline includes individual habits such as prayer, fasting, purity, journaling, and daily devotions. When life gets hectic, the only thing that brings balance is being in the presence of God. He is not the author of confusion; He is the author of peace.

An unbalanced life is God's way of saying, "Seek me."

Once you begin to seek the spirit of God, the personal changes you need to bring balance and peace in your life will be revealed. The spirit will give you insight into things you should let go, or perhaps new things you ought to try.

Today, begin to reflect on things you can do to become more spiritually disciplined. If you are not sure where to start, simply pray and ask God to lead you.

9 Am . . .

GWEN FRANKLIN

You are the one who put me together inside my mother's body,
and I praise you because of the wonderful way you created me.
Everything you do is marvelous! Of this I have no doubt.

PSALM 139:13–14, CEV

I am the one they call when something needs to be done—the right way—with great care and attention to detail. I am the one who catches the vision, the big picture, and breaks it down into pixels to make sure that every player takes his proper place in the scene.

I am Sistah Girl, the strong and steady rock. Everyone, get your piece of the rock! I am the facilitator of a better life for many, and the only life that some have known.

I am the one and only love to that which loves unconditionally, appreciative of greatness and beauty that surely surrounds me. I am the purveyor of hope for the hopeless—and the hopeful. I have been known to encourage the downtrodden, to inspire the uncertain, and to empower willing visionaries. I am the one who gives the subtle shove, throwing down the gauntlet that entices some to reach beyond their visibility into greatness.

Considering all that I am, am I enough? Enough to finish the race that I've been running? Am I still on track? Or have I left the course? I am a thinker who overthinks, a stepper who oversteps, and a facilitator who all too often overcompensates. Through it all, I am a piece of work—in progress.

I am Daughter who pushed past resistance to embrace lessons that were well taught with abundant love. I am Sibling who benefited by observing the hard-line discipline of Brother and Sister. I am Grandchild to four people who grew very old—and very wise.

I am a product of the '70s, when common cause gave youthful expression a platform. I am a sponge to every enlightening theory that illuminates the prospect of a better life—filled with diversity, with a flair for the anomaly. I am a catalyst with an unwavering thirst for change. I am a force, silently heard by those who matter most in the master plan. I am purpose for the purposeless, life for the lifeless, and adventure for those who are willing to take the ride.

I am Mother for the one who will go in my stead, carrying all of the rights of knowledge and wisdom that it is my joy to impart. I am Friend to those who join in my celebrations, my highs, and my lows.

I am proof that Jesus is a healer. Filled with peace, love, joy, and righteousness, I am a child of the king. I am the one that was chosen for this mission . . . by the chosen one. I am a believer, a worshipper, one of His deepest mysteries. I am a miracle. I am a survivor.

A Soul Sister's Guide to Balancing Life with Praise and Prayer

M. GASBY BROWN

 When praise to God occupies a space, nothing else can enter that zone—not depression, sickness, grief, or disappointment. Not jealousy, anger, frustration, confusion, or strife. Since I became a committed Christian and experienced all of these emotional challenges, I say, "Thank you, Lord, for every blessing today," and I start to sing or listen to an uplifting praise song. It works!

Remembering His faithfulness, my spirit soars to a higher level, and I am able to seek God's will for my next hour, my day, and my life. Praise keeps me focused as I reflect on His blessings.

Each day, no matter what, all Christians have a praise report because God sent His son, Jesus Christ, to conquer sin and death by dying on the cross and rising on the third day. He lives! So why can't we, through His power, overcome our challenges and issues? We can and we must if we are to experience the abundant, balanced life that Jesus came to give.

I encourage every soul sister to write and reflect on your blessings for thirty-one days as you recognize God's presence in your life. Praise brings us closer to Him, as He longs to abide in our praise.

Express your heart's desires by writing down your prayer requests. Remember to pray for someone else. How many times have we told people we would pray for them after listening to their challenges and burdens, but when prayer time came we forgot? Pray for yourself and intercede for others. Record your blessings and those of others in a praise report journal. Compile a list of praise songs for each day to hum or sing on your praise and prayer journey.

The power of praise was so important to me as I went through a very painful and unexpected divorce several decades ago that left me broken emotionally and financially. As I was clinging to various "lifelines" that I thought would get me through (people, my education, networking, wine), Jesus clearly spoke to me through a Sunday sermon. He told me to draw closer to Him. I did, through the conduit of praise.

Behavioral experts say that if a person repeats an activity twenty-one consecutive days it becomes a habit. So why not make praise a habit?

I pray that you will be inspired to seek joy in your heart and peace through praise as you see God as "bigger" than anything you face. By the way, I got remarried and all that I lost has been restored twenty-fold. Praise Him!

Be True to Yourself

RONNEAK M. LEE

Nothing brings me greater happiness than to hear that my
children are obeying the truth.

3 JOHN 4, CEV

Although I have only lived a bit over a quarter of
a century, I have had many incredible life experiences, from mind-blowing revelations and in-
explicable mountaintop experiences to painful
experiences that made me want to die because
even my tears could not express my despair.

My biggest spiritual, life, love, and mental
lesson has been: Be true to yourself. So many
folks are struggling with or trying to escape their identity, trying to
commit to promises that no longer work, or staying bound to religion
instead of God, who is still speaking.

Being true to yourself can be the key to living confident, no longer bound, and without self-judgment, and being a powerful example
of self-love and authenticity. What greater joy than to walk in truth—
the truth of who we are, the truth of who God is, and the truth of
that good thing God has called and created us to *be*!

For me, there was no pain greater than to hide in the shadows of
my half-seen and half-lived self. I was constantly allowing others to
pull the proverbial strings of who they thought I should and could be.

Since I am pretty and tall, I was told, "You should be a model." Since I could don a suit and shoes well, and stride gracefully, I was told, "You should be a first lady." Since I appeared happy and always had a smile on my face, I was asked, "What do you have to be depressed about?"

Through my experiences I have learned to be true to myself by silencing the internal judge and the folks who were projecting either their issues or their desires for my life, and by owning and accepting the beautiful enigma of myself.

I've learned to love every part of me—the woman in the mirror with the scars and beauty, the unmet expectations, and the season of incomparable love, and the woman who is loving, free-spirited, spontaneous, funny, daring, and quirky. I love all of me: the teacher and student, the creator and clay, the model and three-point forward, the preacher and first lady, the life giver and the midwife, the minister and the counselee, and much more!

By accepting and loving all of me, being okay with not fitting inside anyone's box, and not limiting myself to who I thought I was or what I wanted yesterday, I am true to myself. It's beautiful. It's transcendent. It's love. It's liberating!

Today, ask yourself: Am I being true to myself? If you are, celebrate you and help to liberate someone else. But if not, start the process today. Look in the mirror and embrace all of you—humanity and divinity. Be open to divine healing, evolution, grace, self-forgiveness, and love! Speak to yourself: "I am beloved, beautiful, and no longer bound!"

The Big Balance Lie

DR. AVIS JONES-DeWEEVER

Do not conform to the pattern of this world, but be
transformed by the renewing of your mind. Then you will be
able to test and approve what God's will is—His good,
pleasing and perfect will.

ROMANS 12:2, NIV

I am a strong Black woman. Who among us
hasn't heard or uttered that phrase? But perhaps in part because of the expectation it de-
notes or the reality to which it bears witness,
Black women especially fall victim to what I
believe to be the "big balance lie."

Certainly, all women struggle with what society tells us should be the optimal balancing
act between our work and our family lives. And many I've come to
know, despite their significant accomplishments as professionals, as
mothers, and as key contributors to their communities, still struggle
with what they believe *should* be, rather than celebrating what *is*.

But Black women, you see, have a very special perspective on this
broader cultural conundrum. For most of us, balance isn't a choice.
It's not something we can turn on and off based on our personal am-
bitions or maternal leanings. No, for us this quest is a perennial and
necessary way of life.

The reality is, in most circumstances we are either the only bread-winner or a critical contributor to our family's bottom line. So for us, addressing this issue of balance is not a theoretical exercise. Nor is it a barometer for where we stand along the feminist continuum. It is a constant, daily reality. And it cannot be ignored.

But hear me, sisters. The idea of balance is a lie. Our lives were never meant to be reduced to such a static notion. Life *is* movement. It is a constant series of evolution—growing, stretching, and constriction. And so instead of reaching for an ideal that is completely counter to the very essence of who we are, it seems we should reach toward an ideal that seeks to fully integrate the various aspects of our lives into one seamless reality.

But still, how do we get there? How do we integrate our varying responsibilities such that we do what we must, while still being there in a meaningful way to live the holistic life that we want?

The answer is threefold.

First, we must get crystal clear about what's most important to us and prioritize our lives around those base notions in real and intentional ways. Far too often, we find it difficult to say no to others' expectations because "it'll only take a second," or perhaps we just don't want to disappoint. But the sooner we realize that diverting attention from our priorities robs us of our ability to live in a manner that reflects what we view as most important, the sooner we'll begin to make the space that's necessary to create a life that is fluid in its integration of those things we hold most dear.

Second, we must live the habit of honesty, especially as it relates to our children. If work makes it unlikely that you'll make each and every sporting event, for example, then pick out two or three and commit to those. If life presents itself so that you can be present at more, then guess who will love the pleasant surprise! But grounding expectations in honesty from the beginning will not dim your light in your child's eyes. In fact, it will only increase his or her understanding and respect for the hard work that you do, and the full person that you are.

And third, get comfortable with seeking and receiving help. So if that means leaning on friends and family for babysitting, meal prep, or other necessities of life, do it!

We must come to the realization that no one can do it all. Now, notice I didn't say that we can't *have* it all. In fact, I believe quite the opposite—that every woman not only can, but *deserves* to have it all. But to get there, we have to learn how to lean on each other in the fulfillment of both our individual and collective dreams.

Showers of Blessings

EYESHA K. MARABLE

My friends, God has made us these promises. So we should
stay away from everything that keeps our bodies and spirits
from being clean. We should honor God and try to be
completely like Him.

2 CORINTHIANS 7:1, CEV

Growing up, my favorite musical group was
Earth, Wind & Fire, particularly their song
"Keep Your Head to the Sky." Ironically, it reminded me of the fourth natural element,
which is not mentioned in the group's name:
water. The message in this song gave me a great
appreciation of water and its significance on
earth. About 71 percent of the planet is made
up of water—oceans, polar ice caps, glaciers, underground aquifers,
wells, lakes, and rivers. Sewers, plants, animals, and humans are full
of it (60 percent of our bodies are made up of water). The rest of the
planet's water is in the sky, as clouds, water vapor, or precipitation.

In my emerging appreciation of water, instead of running for
cover or despising the inconvenience, I began to see rainstorms as
showers of blessings and opportunities for the earth and every crea-
ture within to be cleansed and purified. I was confident, based upon
history, that God would have compassion upon us, that He would

subdue our iniquities and cast all our sins into the depths of the sea (see Micah 7:19). I therefore chose to live a cleaner, refreshed, and purified life, and I encourage you to do the same. Here's how.

Imagine that your parents, teachers, mentors, pastors, counselors, and intercessory prayer partners serve as cleansing agents that remove toxins from your life. When you allow family traditions, sermons, words of wisdom, and tough love to soak in and lather your spirit, they exfoliate the contaminants and begin a deep cleansing process. Abuse of any kind and unfair judgment or treatment can harm us only if we hold on to it. Like layers of dead skin, allow the pain we cause and endure to slough off.

Consider praying every time you shower or wash your hands or your hair, asking God to cleanse your heart, spirit, and mind (Psalm 51:10). As the water saturates your flesh, allow it to rejuvenate your soul, refresh your feelings, and restore your resolve to approach things differently. Ask God, "Purify my soul from _____," as you detail what you expect to go down the drain. Do it with a resolve that all acts of sin endured or committed by thought, word, or deed that would keep you from pursuing your passion and maximizing your potential shall be washed away in that instant. That's right! What goes down a drain cannot be easily retrieved. God wants your unclean thoughts, painful memories, and waste of ill-spoken words and wishes to run down that drain. Give thanks for all uncleanliness being washed away, never to be seen, spoken of, or heard of again.

As with daily showers, remember that the purification process is ongoing, not a onetime event. When time permits, go for a swim in a pool or an ocean, soak in a hot tub or whirlpool, or walk in the rain on a sunny day—and keep your head to the sky.

LOSS

Reflections ❧ *Holes in the Soul*

Life After Loss
DR. CARETHA CRAWFORD

Sisterhood Strength: Loss of Mom and Dad
KIM A. HILL

Dear Grandma
TERI COAXUM

Letting Go
GWEN FRANKLIN

A Sister Speaks About Loss: Five Senses of Grief
DR. CHERYL KIRK-DUGGAN

No One Knows the Day
PHYLLIS PORCHER

Love Always Wins
REV. DIONNE P. BOISSIÈRE, M.DIV.

Have Love and Compassion
ROXANNE M. GIRARD-NESFIELD

A Word
DR. TERESA DELGADO

Reflections ❧ *Holes in the Soul*

Everyone who has lost someone, something, or someplace can agree on one thing. It hurts—deeply—sometimes for hours, days, weeks, or even years. Losing my parents was the most difficult of losses for me. At times, the finality of loss feels overwhelming, yet we must persevere and get to the other side of our pain.

When God instructed Moses to get the people to the other side of the Red Sea, the purpose was for more than symbolism and more than just a victory at that place. God sent them there to model victory for all of us who find ourselves dealing with loss.

Sometimes purpose is birthed out of the pain of loss. Recently, I was with Lucia McBath, also a contributor to this book, who had lost her only child, seventeen-year-old Jordan, to gun violence. His death was as senseless as it as was swift. But from the pain of her loss, Lucy has become an advocate for gun control and is even starring in two movies about it. And although the loss will be with her always, her ministry, Moms Demand Action for Gun Sense in America, is taking lobbying and prayer to an entirely new level.

These pages on loss are touching and encouraging. The stories of these sisters remind us that even in loss, God always comes through. May God, through these writings, lead you beside still waters and restore your soul, as well as the holes within.

Life After Loss

DR. CARETHA CRAWFORD

I tell you for certain that a grain of wheat that falls on the ground will never be more than one grain unless it dies. But if it dies, it will produce lots of wheat.

JOHN 12:24, CEV

I read a book some years ago titled *Gaining Through Losing* (Victor Books, 1982), by Evelyn Christenson. The title itself is enough to cause one to start pulling together and holding tightly to everything valuable. We want to make progress in the journey of life, as very few of us desire to lose anything that is so precious to us. But truth be told, our strengths, courage, hope, people, and things precious to us come at a cost.

I have a wonderful life. I say this now as a sexagenarian, but looking back I'm sure I saw life through different lenses. God has blessed me to fulfill many of my dreams and aspirations. I have traveled extensively, both nationally and internationally. I have dined at fine restaurants, worn elegant clothing, attended events in enviable places, met and greeted a U.S. president. I've lived in my dream home, driven luxury cars, published books, and experienced success in ministry. However, none of these were achieved without paying the high price called "loss."

I lost an infant brother, another brother was killed in an accident, and two others died of illnesses. The loss didn't end there. I also lost a sister to breast cancer, and both of my parents are deceased. With some of these deaths, I was responsible for arranging the funeral services and preaching the eulogy—yes, even my mother's. Despite all this adversity, today I stand strong, thriving in the power of the Lord.

It was God who gave me the strength, strategy, and resolve to forge ahead in my pursuit of destiny. In the midst of the tears, the fears, the uncertainties of life, and the pain, I sought God through prayer, meditation, and reading His Word. I didn't understand His plan, but I held resolutely to His hand and gained insight into who He truly is to me. My faith, trust, knowledge, and understanding of Him grew exponentially.

Seasons of loss require strength, as each death (or the loss of something precious) takes a little wind out of our sails. Resting in the presence of the Lord will renew our strength so we can mount up like the eagle. It's not instant, but little by little, and with God's help, we find the courage to soar again.

Strategy or an action plan is needed to help regain focus on our personal destiny assignments. This personalized strategy is designed to strengthen our commitment to trust Him and make each loss count for the greater good. God is faithful! He will give the guidance that is necessary.

Losing something precious might not be what we desire, but hindsight is twenty-twenty. Oh, what a beautiful sight to behold the things we gain due to loss! Jesus taught that we must lose in order to gain.

> *"Unless a kernel of wheat is planted in the soil and dies, it remains alone. But its death will produce many new kernels— a plentiful harvest of new lives."*
> *(John 12:24, NLT)*

Sisterhood Strength: Loss of Mom and Dad

KIM A. HILL

We often suffer, but we are never crushed. Even when we don't
know what to do, we never give up. In times of trouble, God is
with us, and when we are knocked down, we get up again.

2 CORINTHIANS 4:8–9, CEV

After experiencing a devastating loss, one
might think, "I can't go on." Your heart is broken. Your soul cries, "Why?" and thoughts of
giving up start to envelop your mind. But loss
and heartache are a part of life. Therefore, we
have to be ready to arm ourselves with faith
and hope to turn our sorrow into joy.

It was just before the homegoing celebra-
tion that I saw her. She was lying in that ivory and gold cushioned
casket and I was fuming with anger. Mom, in all her beauty, in all her
greatness, in all her significance, spiritual wisdom, and intellectual
wittiness, was simply reduced to flesh.

Saying that final good-bye to my mother has been one of the hardest things I have ever had to do. A woman of God, a woman filled with
so much life, the matriarch of our family was gone. As disbelief and
depression set in, my only solace was in knowing that Mom's legacy

was one of inner joy. She lived in a way that grace followed her always. She fought the good fight and never gave up. So how could I let this sorrow and pain overwhelm me? I had to live like my mom had lived. I had to lean on my faith and trust that God was with me and had provided me with all I needed to survive this devastating blow. Through prayer with my family and leaning on my sisters, I started to live out Mom's legacy. Joy started to return to my life as I found ways to honor her life and the wonderful woman of God she was.

Not long after my mom's death, another devastating blow hit me. My dad was faced with a health battle that doctors didn't think he could win. My faith would not allow me to accept this diagnosis. Dad needed me and it all became clear: God never gives us more than we can bear. My mom's death, as painful as it was, happened ahead of dad's because I could not have handled both my parents ailing at the same time. My God gave me extra time with my dad to uplift my spirits and bring me joy after my sorrow. Unfortunately, sorrow returned eleven months later.

Losing my dad the day before Mother's Day had to be the most ironic thing I have ever dealt with. How would I now pick myself up again after the team was gone? Affectionately known as my Momzee and Daddy Doo, the loving couple who laughed in the face of sorrow were both gone. But "precious in the sight of the Lord is the death of His saints" (Psalm 116:15, KJV).

My parents were now my angels. Dad had stayed with me long enough to make sure we were all okay. My sisters and I truly leaned on our sisterhood. The sisterly bond, intimate chats, and circle of sisters' prayers carried us through one of the darkest periods of our lives.

> *"For His anger endureth but a moment, and in His favor is life; weeping may endure for a night, but joy cometh in the morning."*
> *(Psalm 30:5, KJV)*

Dear Grandma

TERI COAXUM

I also remember the genuine faith of your mother Eunice. Your
grandmother Lois had the same sort of faith, and I am sure
that you have it as well.

2 TIMOTHY 1:5, CEV

I write now with a heavy heart. Each of your
struggles and sacrifices for me have made me
the person I am today, but you'll never meet
the adult woman you helped to forge. You
won't see my daughters grow more fully into
themselves as women with your virtues, nor
will you know my grandson as he learns the
same lessons you taught me so many years ago.

You were our rock, the glue that kept our family together no matter the challenge. I've shed many tears for you. I miss you, I will always love you, and I offer you my tears of thanksgiving.

> *"The Lord is far from the wicked, but He hears the prayer of*
> *the righteous."*
>   *(Proverbs 15:29, NIV)*

As far back as I remember you were a role model for my brothers
and me. You took us to church weekly. You tithed faithfully, saving

your money in a piece of rag tucked away in your bra. You taught me to honor my commitments, and keep unto the Lord all that is His.

> *"If ye have faith as a grain of mustard seed, ye shall say unto this mountain, Remove hence to yonder place; and it shall remove; and nothing shall be impossible unto you."*
> *(Matthew 17:20, KJV)*

My humble beginnings included my teenage mother being abused by my father, my own premature birth, and our early days without indoor plumbing. Through it all, you showed me how to be thankful and that love is service and devotion. You took me to practices, games, and summer classes, waiting on me for hours. You never taught me to feel sorry for myself or to believe that I was inferior to anyone.

Later, seeking the dreams you knew I could accomplish, I traveled to New York at age sixteen with a box of vanilla wafers, the clothes on my back, and the desire to go to John Jay College of Criminal Justice. A few hours after my arrival, I became homeless. My aunt informed me that I couldn't live with her because she was facing eviction. The Lord and prayer helped me find a place to live with a cousin. I lived there until I was able to find a job and a place of my own.

> *"Christ gives me the strength to face anything."*
> *(Philippians 4:13)*

Thank you for struggling to learn to read the Bible so that you wouldn't be reliant on my grandfather to share the Word with you. Your testimony about things worth working for, your dedication in prayer, and your steadfast courage, humility, and faith were examples that remind me there is no armor I can carry more powerful than knowledge of my Lord and Savior.

I was the first African American deputy state director under Senator Chuck Schumer, and I am currently the regional advocate for

New York, New Jersey, Puerto Rico, and the United States Virgin Islands for the Small Business Administration under President Obama. After earning the first high school diploma and college degree in our family, I've gone on to earn two masters degrees and am planning to pursue my Juris Doctor.

By sharing your stories as I climbed in your bed, you prepared me for a life you never had the ability to live. As a mother and grandmother, I now know how uncertain you must have been. Thank you for your love, dreams, prayer, and example.

Always yours,
Teri

Letting Go

GWEN FRANKLIN

I will bless you with a future filled with hope—a future of success, not of suffering.

JEREMIAH 29:11, CEV

It's 7:23 A.M. I must've slept for ten hours straight! I can't remember the last time that I did that. I guess I can attribute it to that lo-o-o-ng hug, the hard, intense kiss from cheek to cheek, the final good-bye—for now. We both gave the presidential wave—I from the sunroof of the Murano, and he as he walked through the courtyard. There he went, up the steps, slipping through the doors of the dorm that would be his home for the next year. Everything that life had offered over the past eighteen years had led to this point, and culminated in a good night's sleep.

Last year we were searching for colleges. His GPA fell south of 3.0. With cautious optimism we established the position that anything was possible—well, almost anything. We toured New England. In Boston, it was Northeastern, Emerson, Boston University, and Harvard. In Connecticut, Yale. The truth was that I knew he was not going to Harvard—but I thought it important that he see it. Same with Yale.

The search continued. Muhlenberg College, in Allentown, Pennsylvania. Great interview, but short on cultural diversity. Centenary College, in Hackettstown, New Jersey—only as a last resort! Rutgers,

TCNJ (The College of New Jersey), Drew, Rowan—all in New Jersey and all too close to home. I convinced him to take a look at Temple University, in Philly. We walked into the campus arena and saw a sign that read, HOW U DOIN?, compliments of *The Wendy Williams Show*, and boyfriend fell in love with the City of Brotherly Love. I wish they were all that easy! One down.

Next, we went south. I have a great affinity for the South and believed he would develop one, too, if given the opportunity. Morgan State, in Baltimore. No! The city was too violent. University of Maryland, College Park. Now you're talking—huge campus and a nice sequel to Teaneck High. But was it too big? And, oh, those college entrance scores were definitely not cuttin' it!

George Washington University—great reputation, but wrong for my child. And then there was Howard University, my alma mater. I didn't want to push it on him, but I knew it'd make a great fit— environment, grades, and college entrance requirements. Although he'd have to work hard in the first semester of his high school senior year, with a lot of prayer it was attainable.

Fast-forward. Slowly driving away from Drew Hall—down Georgia Avenue, a left onto New York Avenue, and away from the city— there was more joy than the pain of separation. More joy at the notion that he was starting a new phase of his life, probably the most important phase. Setting the stage for his life direction. Making lifelong friends and life-defining choices.

Since his birth, I had poured into him, molded, reshaped, extracted, added, and fine-tuned. Finally, he was at the point where it was time to let go.

I left Washington, D.C.—I-95 North to New Jersey—stopped at my sister's house, and went to sleep!

A Sister Speaks About Loss:
Five Senses of Grief

DR. CHERYL KIRK-DUGGAN

The man replied, "The Scriptures say, 'Love the Lord your God
with all your heart, soul, strength, and mind.' They also say,
'Love your neighbors as much as you love yourself.'"

LUKE 10:27, CEV

 Many sisters experience grief, with various degrees of mindfulness. Some are unconsciously drowning in the loss of relationships, things, expectations, and dreams. When unaware, we often react to others, transferring our pain to them when we are upset with ourselves. Sometimes we self-medicate—food, drugs, alcohol, shopping, gambling, promiscuity, or narcissism. The thirteenth-century mystic Mechthild of Magdeburg claims all desire is desire for God. Thus, only God can soothe the pain of grief.

We must love and work with God-focused people who can help love us into wholeness. Before healing can begin, we can think about grief through our five senses: sight, taste, smell, hearing, and touch.

Sight is perception with our eyes, visual discernment. We can no longer physically see the one we lost to death. With broken relationships, sometimes seeing the person causes agony. When we sit with that pain and analyze the relationship, we can learn to let go of our expectations and assumptions. We can confess our part, and know healing can come when we face and deal with grief. Grief need not destroy us. That which we cannot see, we sometimes taste.

To taste means we experience flavors in the mouth and throat on contact with a substance. The taste of grief can be bitter and acrid, so sharp as to numb our taste buds. That taste can change when we have lived through days and years of loss, and toward healing, in which we genuinely taste the sweet memories. As such, we can "taste and see the goodness of the Lord" (Psalm 34:8). Taste closely relates to smell.

Smell involves the power of perceiving scents via nasal organs. When we smell grief, we can inhale odors of loss and death, of things diminished and gone. Some overpowering smells make us so sick and overwhelmed. Yet when the pain dissipates we smell the sweet generosity of love.

Like smell, the sense of hearing affects us in powerful ways. We hear as we perceive with our ears the sound made by someone or something. The sounds of grief and loss range from dead silence to whimpers to moans and wailing, our reactions to deep loss. During such times, people often reach out to touch us.

Touch means we come so close to something or someone as to come into contact; to handle, manipulate, or alter something or someone. The first touch of grief and loss can be repulsive and frightening—for some, a new, horrible space.

For others grief is as ancient as time. They have never dealt with the first loss and the losses become compounded. Experiences of loss, death, dying, and grief remind us that life is a gift and to savor each moment. When bad things happen, we need to give ourselves permission to experience our feelings so that we do not become paralyzed, the living dead.

God is with us as we walk through grief. We can be whole again.

No One Knows the Day

PHYLLIS PORCHER

I come to you, Lord, for protection. Don't let me be ashamed.
Do as you have promised and rescue me. Listen to my prayer
and hurry to save me. Be my mighty rock and the fortress
where I am safe. You, Lord God, are my mighty rock and my
fortress. Lead me and guide me, so that your name will be
honored.

PSALM 31:1–3, CEV

On a snowy evening in February 1983, my
mother, forty-seven years old, left this world behind. I was fifteen.

She was mother not only to my older brother
and me but also to many others, so her passing
was far reaching. I'm not dramatic like my
daughter. She says if anything ever happens to
me, she'll "wild out," just not care anymore.

For the record, when this happened to me I was already dealing
with other concerns, such as esteem issues and feelings of being left
alone. And now, my provider, my caregiver was gone. Not gone as in
on a trip somewhere, but gone. Period.

What did I do? I withdrew. I became distant from everyone, even
immediate family, for a long time. Looking back, I really needed help;

and yes, people offered help, but I believe my mental health suffered. I became depressed, withdrawn, and just plain odd. I was suffering and I kept myself in this state, which is never good.

I would watch people whose mothers were still present, and feel my loss even more. I became resentful and jealous, angry that my mother wasn't here anymore. I felt I didn't have anyone to talk to. There was a neighbor whose mother died giving birth. I wondered if we had a connection.

I just turned forty-seven this year. One thing I did learn through my mother's death is to take good care of my health—physical and mental. My mother was a smoker and I smoked for twenty-five years. I've learned to avoid certain things for the sake of longevity. That's important to me because, God willing, I would like to be here another forty or fifty years.

This is hard. I almost passed on this project because I didn't want to go back into the feelings and the remembering. But I'm doing it, and it's really not bad at all. I thought about it. There's a person now whom I'm comforting about the loss of their mother a few months prior. She comes to me and cries and asks if it will get better. I told her, yes. It does get better, but it takes time and work.

I am grateful to my paternal grandmother. She came and stayed with me for two years after my mother passed. She kept cheer about her. A Jehovah's Witness, she was strong with her faith, so it was a blessing she chose to be with me. I was a sad soul, not talking to anyone if I could help it. But she stayed with me, warming me up and imploring me to be a part of things, saying, "No man is an island." And it's true; people make the world go round.

It's important to live well, because as cliché as it sounds, no one knows the day or the hour. Once I understood that, due to the deaths of other people, I applied this saying to myself.

In hindsight, I have learned a lot. Looking forward, I still have a lot to learn. My daughters have taught me, shaped me into this mother I am today. I give thanks for them. For all their drama, the trials they've put me through, I give thanks. I did the same for my own mother. We all do.

Please remember, if you've lost your mother, you are not alone. It is painful and brings darkness to you, but the sun will return to your life.

Love Always Wins

REV. DIONNE P. BOISSIÈRE, M.DIV.

> I am sure that nothing can separate us from God's love—
> not life or death, not angels or spirits, not the present or the
> future, and not powers above or powers below. Nothing in
> all creation can separate us from God's love for us in Christ
> Jesus our Lord!
>
> ROMANS 8:38–39, CEV

In March 2012, I experienced one of the most devastating losses in my adult life. It led to an extended time of grief, depression, self-doubt, and confusion, and a severe onset of health and financial challenges, some of which I am still battling today. I lost my job—my vocation—and what seemed to be my life! I was violently forced out of a place that I deeply loved and held in sacred regard. I loved it almost more than I loved myself.

The loss and disenfranchisement of grief was overwhelming, yet just the beginning of many more tragic losses that I would have to endure. For two years I was unemployed, and for the better half of that, I was without health benefits. I underwent hospitalization and an invasive surgical procedure, and I survived the threat of cervical cancer, the loss of a lifelong friendship, and the death of five members of my family over the last six months of that two-year span.

Convinced that I had lost everything—even the favor and love of God that I had come to understand would always be mine—I saw an impossible battle in my mind so enormous, I knew I could never win. Why didn't God love me enough to protect me from pain, hurt, disease, and loss? I asked myself this question repeatedly. As with each loss, it seemed as though my soul died a bit more each day.

One day, I was studying Scripture, searching for some glimmer of hope, and came across the text I'd read at Rev. Dr. Ella P. Mitchell's homegoing/funeral service several years ago. She was a matriarch and mentor for many Black clergywomen nationally and internationally. It was as if God spoke directly to me in her voice and read these divine words aloud to breathe life back into me so that my soul would live again.

Paul spoke to the followers of Jesus in Rome in this passage and made clear his declaration to hold fast to the promises God made to those who were in Christ. There was no persecution too great, no power on earth or above, no tribulation or hard times, no created thing real or imagined that could separate them from the love that God had for them.

This is still true for Christ's followers. We are reminded that God's love is stronger than any power that may attempt to hinder us from becoming who we were created to be. I have learned that there is no job, career, or vocation that can define me. I see the God in me and *she* is beautiful! And no matter how deep the pain or loss, the battle is not too difficult for the Creator.

Though it may sound clichéd, there is indeed an eternal fight between good and evil, between love and hate. But I, too, am persuaded that there is one who will fight for us and who cannot lose. God is love . . . and love always wins!

Have Love and Compassion

ROXANNE M. GIRARD-NESFIELD

Be the teacher of your heart; do not allow your heart to
become your teacher.

BUDDHIST PROVERB

I lost my mother just shy of her eighty-fifth
birthday this past year. She had been living
with me for the previous fifteen years, since my
father's death in 1999. She was a small Japanese
woman, no taller than four feet, five inches,
who spoke broken English and had limited
reading and writing skills.

I was grateful she'd lived so long. You can
say she had a full life. She was born in Japan in 1929. She was a practicing Buddhist her whole life. She married an American soldier and
they moved to the United States in 1958. She was married for forty-
five years, until my father's death. She raised two daughters who gave
her three grandchildren. She lived her last years in San Diego, but she
had also lived in Arizona, Illinois, Georgia, and Florida while in the
United States.

I have many fond memories of my mother. She taught me many
lessons about life.

The biggest lesson I learned from my mother as I remember her
each day was how she became such a strong woman and had a heart

full of love. Her childhood was devastating. Her family was very poor. She was sold as a child to another family to work on a farm; as a result, she had only a fifth-grade education. She survived the war and the dropping of the atomic bomb on her country, which claimed the life of her father and separated her from her siblings and family members.

She would finally find and reunite with her younger sister forty years later. After the war, she relocated to Tokyo to find work, where she met a young American soldier and fell in love. Life was not easy for her, being with an American. Like many other Japanese "war brides," she was shunned by countrymen, friends, and even family. Making life even more difficult, she moved to a new country with her husband, without speaking the language or knowing the customs.

She arrived unwelcomed by many Americans, who still possessed hateful feelings from the war. These included some of her husband's family members. She experienced discrimination and many hurtful encounters throughout her life because she was Japanese. Despite all of this, she learned the language and customs and raised her two daughters (after two miscarriages). She was determined to live the American dream.

As a child, I did not see all of this going on in her life. What I saw was a mom who would help anyone in need. She would cook meals for people, watch their children, and offer to clean their homes, all while taking public transit everywhere because she could not drive a car. She would lend money to those in need, even though she and my father struggled financially because they did not make a lot of money. She had no fear to speak to everybody she met, even with her broken English. She went to night classes to become a U.S. citizen, and she learned how to drive a car at age fifty-five.

She taught her heart to love and be strong. I received her love every day of my life, and so did the people she met during her life. In spite of her childhood and struggles in life, she remained strong and did not allow her heart to become bitter and negative. So when I catch myself starting to complain about my problems and inconveniences, I now pause to remember her strength. I try to be strong like my mom. I try to teach my heart to have love, compassion, and patience. After all, my mother was able to do this for eighty-five years.

A Word

DR. TERESA DELGADO

In the beginning was the one who is called the Word. The
Word was with God and was truly God. From the very
beginning the Word was with God. And with this Word, God
created all things. Nothing was made without the Word.
Everything that was created received its life from Him, and
His life gave light to everyone. The light keeps shining in the
dark, and darkness has never put it out.

JOHN 1:1–5, CEV

The way out is to tell:
Speak of the acts perpetrated upon us,
Speak the atrocities
Speak the injustices
Speak the personal violations of the soul
Someone will listen
Someone will believe our stories
Someone will join us.

FROM CHARLOTTE PIERCE-BAKER,
Surviving the Silence: Black Women's Stories of Rape
(W. W. NORTON & COMPANY, 2000)

There is a power and presence in voices rising, whether in song or protest, preaching or teaching. There is a power in the spoken word, and in the silence between the words spoken.

I reflect upon the immense power of the word as I write this on the day the Christian community remembers the Holy Innocents, *los inocentes*, when Herod sought to wipe out the threat of the child born in Bethlehem who had been proclaimed to him by the wise men of the East.

At the same time, another word is spoken, by the angel of the Lord in a dream to Joseph—to take Mary and the child to safety in Egypt—and to the wise men not to return to Herod.

> *"A voice was heard in Ramah,*
> *wailing and loud lamentation,*
> *Rachel weeping for her children;*
> *she refused to be consoled, because they are no more."*
> (Matthew 2:18, HCSB)

Thus claimed the prophetic word of Jeremiah, and I cannot help but think of all the mothers who are today weeping for their children who are no more: the mothers of Michael Brown, Eric Garner, Tamir Rice, Yvette Smith, Andy Lopez, Miriam Carey, Reynaldo Cuevas, Rekia Boyd, Aiyana Jones, Tarika Wilson, and too many others. What word of consolation can they be given to ease their brokenness, their pain?

And what can I tell my own brown children, two daughters and two sons, my African–Puerto Rican babies, about the world they venture out into every day? About the injustices, atrocities, and violations of the soul and body they will experience by virtue of the skin they are in?

All I can do is offer this prayer, invoking the power of the Word that gives life and hope, that propels our collective voice, in song and protest, preaching and teaching, to inspire all of us, with fierce courage, to change the world:

> In this moment of endless sorrow,
> In our grief and mourning too deep for words,
> We invoke the one who, in the beginning, spoke the
>   Word and was the Word,
> The Word who was made flesh,
> The Word whose flesh was beaten and bloodied,
>   violated and torn,
> The Word was broken, yet the Word was spoken.
> Silence the clamor, to hear the silenced into speech,
> To speak a word, to tell a story of stories, of the children
>   who are no more.
> Open our ears to the words of brokenness,
> The words of suffering,
> The words of hope.
> Give us the tears to cry:
> Tears of anger, of rage, of defiance,
> Tears of healing.
> Embolden us with the courage
> To act in the world,
> To work for justice,
> To speak a broken word, out of broken flesh.
> In the beginning was the Word
> And the Word was made flesh
> And the Word and flesh is all we have
> And you have taught us, it is all we need
> To heal our broken world.

SISTERHOOD

Reflections & Let Me Break the Alabaster Box for You

Sisterhood
TERRY B. WILLIAMS

Words for the Sisterhood
REV. DR. GLORIA E. MILLER

Keep Shining On: A Letter to My Sisters
JUDY MALANA

Reflections ❧ *Let Me Break the Alabaster Box for You*

My first glimpse into the bonds of adult sisterhood came from being around a lot of strong, beautiful Black women who were blood sisters and cousins to each other. My mother was left orphaned and alone from a family of nine brothers and sisters, so her cousins were her sisters. I saw how close they were and the loving bond they shared, aunts and cousins loving each other. When we would take trips to the South during the summer, I would have an opportunity to see how my relatives got along both intra- and interfamily. As the women shared in the kitchen, laughing and talking as they prepared meals and discussed children, husbands, church, and a variety of other topics, I came to recognize that sisterhood extends beyond bloodlines.

At church, my mother was part of a group of thirteen women who were known as the "inner circle." They all became my godmothers, loving me individually and collectively. This intimate circle of sisterhood worshipped together on Sundays, and then socialized together after church was over. They also hung out together during the week. As with my extended family, this group of women shared stories as they did the work of the church, bonded by faith and friendship. They were as close as blood sisters might be and they were a joy to be around when they got together.

One of my closest sisterly bonds evolved when I met Yolanda King, daughter of slain civil rights leader Martin Luther King Jr. and

Coretta Scott King. When we met, we hit it off right away. Our introduction came through my late brother Charles, who was then a member of the New York General Assembly. Yolanda was trying to find her path as a young woman in her twenties, and she had arranged to intern with my brother for a summer. His office was just a block from my home, so I crafted an excuse to go over and meet her.

Yolanda and I got along so well because we had many things in common. We were both into drama. We both were in school in Massachusetts—she was at Smith College and I was at Emerson. We both were engaged in the arts and communications. She was an actress. We were only about a year apart in age, so we started hanging out together.

The bond of our sisterly friendship was sealed during an eight-week backpacking trip we took through Africa. Yolanda really wanted to visit the motherland, but Mrs. King was very conservative and had great reservations about her daughter going on such a trip. I had already visited Africa the year before with Operation Crossroads Africa. I convinced Mrs. King that I knew the continent very well and that I had enough contacts to get us anything we might need while over there.

As a mother, I now understand her concern. Yolanda and I were only about nineteen years old at the time. We considered ourselves smart, mature young women, but mothers see things differently. But on the strength of my assurance, Mrs. King gave her consent for Yolanda to go. We covered nine countries with nothing but our backpacks, duffel bags, and mountain boots.

We weren't a part of any organized group. It was just the two of us and we had to depend on each other. We had a few challenges, but God was watching over us. One day we were put off of a bus and left in the desert. We were searched in ways that made us uncomfortable. We had to combine our strengths to make it through the eight weeks. We had to learn how to bond.

Yolanda was a night owl and I was and still am an "early to bed, early to rise" type of person. Somehow we made things work despite our different sleep patterns. Some places where we stayed had trains that came in only once a week. If we missed one, we would be stuck in that town for an entire week. Resolving that we had fifty-six days together and we could make the trip either fun or miserable, we chose to work together and have fun. At times we would crack up like giggly little girls. Through that trip we knew we were sisters.

The Lord was watching over us, but so was Mrs. King with her watchful mother's eye. We had some trouble in Lagos, Nigeria. Thankfully, one of the wealthy chiefs there was a friend of Mrs. King. He took care of us and flew us home on a Concorde jet. Those eight weeks bonded us like nothing else could. That trip, our mutual love of theater, and our love for our people made us sisters.

When I think of our friendship I am reminded that bonds are not determined by how much time you spend with a person. As Yolanda and I grew older, our career paths would take us in many different directions, yet we remained close, even when we didn't see each other often.

I count my blessings for the sisterhood I shared with Yolanda, and it came abruptly to an end with her untimely passing in 2007. In an instant my sister-friend of thirty years was gone. The year before she died, we were blessed to be in the same city simultaneously on three or four different occasions. We were both delighted to see each other so often.

Yolanda and I were bonded by our similarities as well as our differences. We didn't have a biological bond, like Mary and Martha in the Bible, but we definitely shared the bond of love and the blood of Jesus that made us as close as two sisters could be.

We may never know what bonds women together in sisterhood— shared experiences, shared joys, shared lifestyles, and even shared miseries. We have often bonded through our mutual oppression. In the book and the movie *The Help*, the women who worked as domestics were bonded by their common experience of low wages, low respect, and low social standing. They frequently commiserated, but very often shared in humorous and loving moments.

Women inspire each other through acts of sisterhood great and small. In *Sister to Sister*, the book I edited in 1988, one story of sisterhood has stayed in my heart. Activist Ramona Edelin shared a story called "A Sisterly Celebration," recounting how a number of close friends had been invited to her home for a birthday celebration.

In the midst of a day that was supposed to celebrate her, Ramona used it to bless others and remembered her newest neighbor, a young woman who was a new mother. Ramona invited her to the party to engage in the communion of women gathered there. Rather than receiving a gift from her neighbor, Ramona gave her the gift of fellowship.

I call such deeds an act of "Let me break the alabaster box for you. Let me help you." Throughout history women have broken the alabaster boxes of future generations. One group of women who impressed me this way is the founders of Delta Sigma Theta Sorority, Inc. Just a few days after they organized in 1913 as a sorority committed to public service, their first act was to participate in the women's suffrage march in Washington, D.C. They joined in solidarity with the white organizers, even though they were forced to march at the back of the line. They were breaking the alabaster box of hundreds of thousands of African American young women who would come after them.

I'd wanted to be a part of the sorority all my life, but events had just never come together for that to happen. I liked Delta Sigma Theta's strong social action stance, so I watched from a distance. I believe we move by assignment and by opportunity, but I was still floored when I was invited to become an honorary member. My invitation was extended by then–national president Cynthia Marie Antoinette Butler-McIntyre. I readily accepted and I've never looked back. It's been a joy to experience sisterhood on a large scale through the sorority as I meet other members from coast to coast. Delta is the largest of all Black sororities, with more than three hundred thousand initiated members, so I run into sisters everywhere I go.

Through Delta and through other relationships, I have learned that sisterhood is not always about huge acts; rather, it's about simple acts of kindness. Many of the honorary members have bonded in sisterhood among ourselves. It's a blessing to have sisterly relationships with women such as Lisa Jackson, Angela Bassett, Sheryl Lee Ralph, and Suzzanne Douglas. Many sorors have offered to volunteer and work on my campaign for the House of Representatives and a soror is helping me edit this book.

Delta Sigma Theta is a predominantly Black sorority, and I think there is often a special bond among women of color, perhaps because we go through so much. Still, I have been blessed to link heart-to-heart with women of every race and ethnicity in the bond of sisterhood.

Sisterhood Is as Old as the Bible

The stories we read of Mary and Martha in the Bible show that like many other sisters, they are often together. They disagreed, as when Martha complained to Jesus that Mary should have been helping her in the kitchen instead of sitting around (presumably with the men) listening to His teaching. One sister was better able to deal with her grief than the other.

Martha may have been the older of the two. She exhibited the characteristics of an older sister. Luke 10:38 tells us that she invited Jesus into her home, so perhaps she was regarded as the mistress of the house. While Jesus was their houseguest, Martha was more concerned about being a good hostess and fulfilling her responsibilities. Then, when their brother, Lazarus, died (John 11), Martha went out to meet Jesus and tell Him what had happened, while Mary languished inside, too consumed with grief to greet their miracle-working friend.

The Bible gives us many wonderful examples of sisterhood—Naomi and Ruth, Mary and Martha, and the other women who followed Jesus throughout Galilee. They formed a bond as women who were free enough to follow Christ rather than convention. They were determined to go to Jesus's tomb and anoint His body, even though they had no way to roll back the heavy stone that had been placed in front of them.

Powerful things happen when women bond and band together. The men of Persia knew the danger of women forming a bond around an issue, as evidenced by King Xerxes's advisers urging him to deal swiftly with his rebellious queen before all the women started to emulate her behavior.

Women in the Black Church bonded, very often emulating the biblical women who preceded them. Mother boards in the church were matriarchs who provided oversight to the younger women of the church, guiding them in their mission service while giving them wisdom to grow in life and in spirit. The mother board would offer consolation to young women who became pregnant without the benefit of marriage. These sage women would offer comfort and encouragement to young women whose husbands had roving eyes or counsel others on appropriate church attire. They might donate from their meager resources to help a student struggling to go back to college. Their methods may have seemed stern at times, but their actions were rooted in sisterly love.

Organized groups of church matriarchs are withering in the Black Church, and we must wonder who will reach out to the many young women today who lack a strong maternal influence. We never grow too old for sister-mothers and sister-aunts, and their absence from our lives often shows in the choices we make. Perhaps the Samaritan woman Jesus encountered at the well might have stopped short of five husbands and a lover if she'd had the benefit of close female relationships (John 4). Apparently she had no female friends and sought affirmation and validation through her relationships with men. She drew her water from the community well during the heat of the day because that was more tolerable than the hot scorn of the women who gathered there in the early morning hours.

The Samaritan woman may be our poster child for what happens to us when we lack strong female bonds. Someone said a sister-friend is the first person you call when you're in trouble, but the last person you want to call because you know she's going to let you have it when she comes to rescue you. But even that is a part of the enigmatic formula of sisterhood that perpetually confounds the male gender while it continues to fortify us.

Sisterhood

TERRY B. WILLIAMS

Most important of all, you must sincerely love each other,
because love wipes away many sins. Welcome people into your
home and don't grumble about it. Each of you has been blessed
with one of God's many wonderful gifts to be used in the
service of others. So use your gift well.

I PETER 4:8–10, CEV

The tumultuous climate of the world today exists because we've lost *sisterhood*. Women are the nurturers and the glue that holds everything together, but because of greed, jealousy, and envy we are fragmented. This brokenness has had a domino effect on each generation behind us and has led to the world being in chaos. When women do nothing, everything falls apart.

From 1964 to 2005, we had a dynamic sister who started her sisterhood movement with everyday women in the 1960s, former congresswoman Shirley Chisholm. She was the first African American woman elected to Congress, the first major party Black candidate for president of the United Sates, and the first woman to run for the Democratic presidential nomination. This sister was instrumental in securing unemployment benefits for domestic workers; the SEEK Program (Search for Education, Elevation, and Knowledge), which gives disadvantaged students a chance to enter college; and the Special Supplemental Nutrition Program for Women, Infants, and Children (WIC). She also cofounded the National Women's Political Caucus. We failed ourselves and Shirley Chisholm by not joining forces with her.

Now we have another sister, Ambassador Suzan Johnson Cook, heading a sisterhood movement, ProVoice/ProVoz. Let us provide for a better future not only for our young but also for our elders and ourselves, for we are *alive*.

Words for the Sisterhood

REV. DR. GLORIA E. MILLER

The body of Christ has many different parts, just as any other
body does.

I CORINTHIANS 12:12, CEV

Ubuntu: "I am, because of you."

During the time of Nelson Mandela's
death, I listened to many hours of commentary
reflecting on his life. I learned he was fondly
called "Mabida" in his native land. I was also
introduced to the term *ubuntu*. This was one of
Nelson Mandela's favorite sayings after having
been imprisoned for twenty-seven years. The
word means, "I am, because of you."

I reflected on the word from two perspectives. The first was how it
relates to the sisterhood and how interconnected we are regardless of
our position, race, or creed. And in order for the sisterhood not to just
survive but to strive and even flourish, we have to operate in an authentic spirit of community whose members care for each other. In a
real sense, sisterhood is not about the titles we hold; rather, it is about
the ties we build with each other. It's about building authentic relationships in which trust, integrity, and loyalty are at the forefront as
we interact.

Sisterhood is about relationships that help us to be aware that we are connected as links in a chain to one another. If one link in the chain is not fortified, the chain becomes weak and eventually will break or will fail to function as it was designed. To put it another way, we must work hard to keep each link in the sisterhood chain strong and healthy.

So the questions become: How do we keep each link in the chain healthy and whole? How do we value what every sister brings to the table? I would like to suggest that we can intentionally interact with each other in ways that demonstrate that we value, respect, and honor one another.

To take this one step further we can ask ourselves several more questions: How does what I say impact my sister? How about what I do? How does what I don't say matter? How does what I don't do affect my sister? How would I feel if what I said or what I did was done to me? How mindful am I that I am my sister's keeper? The old adage is still true: Action speaks louder than words.

My second reflection on the word *ubuntu* bought me to thoughts of the Scripture passage in 1 Corinthians 12:12: We are one body with many parts. In order for the body to function properly, it must be supported and all of its parts cared for as the whole. We can't dismiss any part if we want to be healthy and strong.

We survive, we strive, and we flourish together. Individually, we make up the whole. As Nelson Mandela said to his nation: "*Ubuntu*— I am, because of you."

As the sisterhood we can say to each other, I need you to survive. "I am, because of you!"

Keep Shining On: A Letter to My Sisters

JUDY MALANA

Make your light shine, so that others will see the good that you
do and will praise your Father in heaven.

MATTHEW 5:16, CEV

 My dearest sisters,

Thank you.
Thank you for who you are.
Thank you for stepping out on a journey of faith.
Maybe you didn't always know it, but I have
looked to you for encouragement.
When my own spiritual path wasn't so clear,
I would lift my head and see you.
You have set the example for me, and so many others.
Whatever you have set your mind on, you have accomplished.
From dreaming new dreams, to redefining yourself, to shattering
stereotypes,
You have allowed the grace of God to move through you in
magnificent ways.
Even when critics assailed, you stood firm.
When God opened doors for you, some minds remained closed
Yet you remained strong—not shackled by the prejudice of
others.

When obstacles came, you pushed through
Never allowing the walls of self-doubt or fear to enclose you.
You never wavered from your calling.
You created sacred spaces in chaotic places
Even when the cell phone didn't stop ringing or the laundry
    remained undone,
Or when a sister needed someone to chat with awhile.
You found refuge in positive relationships
And not in places for pity parties or tirades.
Each and every time, the Lord was with you.
Phenomenal. Yes, you are.
From your inner strength to your fashion sense and fresh
    "mani-pedi,"
Your beauty illuminates the darkest night.
Keep shining on, my dear sisters.
You were not meant to stand in the shadows of others, but to
Radiate the light God has given you.
Continue to trail-blaze. You are not alone.
As doors of opportunity open, continue to walk through them.
There is no one and nothing that can stifle your steps.
Not when your sisters have your back.
Yes, we are all on the sacred path together.
Look around; we are there.
The color of our skin, the texture of our hair, and the shape of
    our hips
Do not matter—for we are all sisters
United by the spirit in a courageous journey of faith and action.
We are proving our critics wrong,
Pushing back against micro-inequities, micro-aggressions, and
    micro-minded mentalities.
We are letting our light shine on to the glory of God.
Our time to exhale will come when we no longer have to justify
    our place

On the field, at the table, or in the boardroom.
Our victory is not ours alone, but belongs to our children and
    our children's children.
My dear sisters, we need each other.
The road ahead is uncharted, and the journey is fierce, but
God's grace is moving and working among us.
The synergy of our sisterhood is greater than the sum of our
    individual efforts.
And it is awesome.

Love and peace,
A sister in Christ

AGING

Reflections ❦ *Changing Seasons*

Aging Mindfully
JOANN STEVENS

Aging Grace
CHAPLAIN VIRGINIA JACKSON

In the Beauty of Holiness
LITA GAITHERS

Live in the Moment
MERCEDES NESFIELD

Reflections ❧ *Changing Seasons*

Well, it's here and there's no turning back. It started with that invitation to AARP that came in the mail on your fiftieth birthday. The reality sets in and you realize that you have become the older, "seasoned" woman you used to point to and talk about.

But along the way you get the clues. It may be the slow motion of getting out of a car, or the bones that start hurting just before it rains, or the liniment you have to put on before bed, or the pills you have to take once you get out of bed. Maybe you woke up hurting for no apparent reason. Perhaps you can no longer tolerate dairy products or spicy foods. You may be losing hair on your head and growing it in places you were never meant to have hair, like your chin. It's all real, sisters. But how we are helped to and through the aging process, or dealing with those around us who are, is what this chapter will help with.

I remember when my late mother's season changed. I was so used to her jumping out of the car and getting her own packages and prescriptions, until one day she said, "I just can't." Sobering.

Seasons. We all must face them. But then there are many who embrace their aging, who actually seem to become more agile. Others dare to take advantage of their courage and continue to dream and dare. Some women experience a tremendous sense of freedom as they grow older, and find the courage to do things they feared risking previously. They do amazing things—take, for example, Mercedes

Nesfield, who seems ageless. She travels with me from K Street in Washington, D.C., to Kosovo, on the other side of the globe, and Lattice Graham (and others), who swims with me in the Harlem Honeys and Bears synchronized swim team. And it is she who reminds me that it's really all right.

There is no fountain of youth, despite what the beauty product manufacturers want us to believe. There is only one alternative to growing older, so we should make the best of the time that we have. And as we become older, we can reflect on the carefree or even foolish days of our youth. Hopefully we will look on them with fondness and gratitude and smile knowingly. The things we did in our youth are rarely the things we regret. It's the things we failed to do.

As long as we are blessed to live, we should rejoice at growing older, despite our aches and pains and medications. We can be happy that we can hold a younger woman by the hand and mentor her through certain challenges. We can celebrate the wisdom that comes with getting some years under our belts.

Aging in Western culture is often difficult because we glorify youth, but in many other nations, the elderly hold a place of honor. Among our more than five hundred Native American nations, each has its own traditions and attitudes toward aging and elderly care. But in many tribal communities, elders are respected for their wisdom and life experiences. Within many Native families, elders are expected to pass down teachings to younger family members. In many Asian and Indian cultures as well, elder members command great respect.

Let's deal with aging. Age gracefully and wear it as a badge of honor. Age joyfully, knowing that you are a survivor who persevered where so many others have fallen away. Age thankfully, glad for the lessons learned, for the courage found, and for the wisdom gleaned. When you can look at the beauty of your aging self from within, you will look in the mirror and see the outer beauty that is you as well.

Aging Mindfully

JOANN STEVENS

Later, I will give my Spirit to everyone. Your sons and
daughters will prophesy. Your old men will have dreams,
and your young men will see visions.

JOEL 2:28, CEV

Some years ago I lost a relative in his twenties
to the ravages of urban life and poverty. He was
the victim of an abusive father and an emotionally damaged mother, and he had a need for
gratifications that destroyed his body and life.

As we talked in the hospital during his final
days, I remember asking him about his greatest
desire.

"To have long life," he answered.

"You can have eternal life," I said. "There's nothing longer than
that."

Popular culture often glorifies fast and furious living among
youth while painting aging as a woeful inheritance of an old mind
and body that you prop up with herbal supplements, exercise, and
cosmetic surgery.

Thank God aging has taught me better.

The creaky joints, gray hair, and "senior moments" are there. But
if you age mindfully, so is the inner peace of self-acceptance, wisdom

earned from experience, and the knowledge that you can count on yourself.

Time has given me a broad and deep education, but spiritual mindfulness and being raised to have an open, teachable spirit have helped create the foundation that has forged my faith and trust in God.

Proverbs 29:18 (CEV) proclaims, "Without guidance from God, law and order disappear, but God blesses everyone who obeys His Law." The more popular King James version reads, "Where there is no vision, the people perish: but he that keepeth the law, happy is he."

We age from the moment we are born, living out days numbered by God. Some people, like my relative, lack vision and aren't raised to age well or productively. Untaught or unteachable, they live broken lives of shattered hopes and unspoken dreams.

Spiritual mindfulness can help guide a teachable spirit to fulfillment as we age, and provide understanding that aging is not only a measure of how long we live but also a testimony declaring how well we are living under God's guidance and grace.

For me, aging has become a journey of adventure and discovery, a trek of spiritual mindfulness, of repentance and restoration, in which I have traded rehearsed hurts, resentments, and regrets for an attitude of gratitude, humility, and love.

The older I get the clearer I see God's blessings in aging. I am thankful for the spiritually mindful women of diverse ages, ethnicities, religions, and backgrounds that He has sent my way to help illuminate dark pathways, offer shelter in storms, and provide sisterhood in times of celebration.

In appreciation of Him and them, I commit to using my gifts of aging to support sisters young and old, to encourage play relatives and blood relatives, longtime friends, and fleeting acquaintances with the gifts of love, patience, and spiritual wisdom that maturation has provided to me.

With the Holy Spirit's help, may these gifts ease burdens and inspire fruitful visions of long, well-lived lives.

> *"Later, I will give my Spirit to everyone. Your sons and*
> *daughters will prophesy. Your old men will have dreams, and*
> *your young men will see visions."*
> *(Joel 2:28, CEV)*

Aging Grace

CHAPLAIN VIRGINIA JACKSON

We never give up. Our bodies are gradually dying, but we ourselves are being made stronger each day. These little troubles are getting us ready for an eternal glory that will make all our troubles seem like nothing. Things that are seen don't last forever, but things that are not seen are eternal. That's why we keep our minds on the things that cannot be seen.

2 CORINTHIANS 4:16–18, CEV

As I celebrated my seventy-third birthday on February 3, 2015, I was inspired to share what has been the most profound and rich experience of my life. Of the many lessons learned, the most important has been to remain teachable as I grow in grace. To walk by faith, remembering to live in the awareness of the presence of the eternal moment by moment, realizing each day that it is not by might or by power, but rather by the spirit of the Lord that it all gets done.

As the outer appearance changes with time, the signs of aging become evident as hair grays, wrinkles appear, skin sags, eyesight dims, and steps shorten. Scripture tells us that there is something of greater value and importance happening simultaneously on the inside. "Therefore we do not lose heart. Though outwardly we are wasting away, yet inwardly we are being renewed day by day. For our light and momentary troubles are achieving for us an eternal glory that far outweighs them all. So we fix our eyes not on what is seen, but on what is unseen, since what is seen is temporary, but what is unseen is eternal" (2 Corinthians 4:16–18, NIV).

How exciting it is to grow in grace and wisdom as we, from time to time, eat of the bread of adversity and drink of the water of affliction along the way! We have the blessed assurance that our loving and powerful Lord gives us the opportunity to live through them for a reason. Our learning possibilities are limited only to the degree of our willingness to be teachable.

I received a phone call in 1987 that gave me an opportunity to grow through a horrific event. The voice on the other end of the line informed me that my dear father had been brutally murdered. I remember my words as I looked up to the sky: "God must have something of great importance for me to do that I needed this experience."

Through the pain and loss of that tragedy I learned how to minister, with passion, to people in crisis from a very real and personal place of experience. This lesson has been extremely beneficial to me as a chaplain providing spiritual care for our nation's veterans.

In the Beauty of Holiness

LITA GAITHERS

Christ did this, so that He would have a glorious and holy church, without faults or spots or wrinkles or any other flaws.
EPHESIANS 5:27, CEV

> Wrinkles, wrinkles, on my face
> Tells me that soon I'll be leaving this place
> Graying hairs, sagging breasts
> Try to keep me from feeling my best
> Wrinkles, wrinkles, on my face
> Soon I'll be leaving this dwelling place.

As I look at myself in the mirror each day and see my aging body, it helps me to stay focused on the big picture. My soul and spirit are eternal, but my body is not. There'll come a time when my soul and spirit will separate from this corruptible covering and be given a beautiful, incorruptible eternal form.

My wrinkles may reflect that I'm over fifty, but my soul tells me that I'm as creative, imaginative, and inventive as any thirty-year-old. My heart may get tired of pumping one day and stop, but my spirit has the will to live forever and never miss a precious moment.

So with great anticipation, I'm able to cheerfully look forward to aging and death without fear, because of the blessed hope in Christ. I can see past the wrinkles and the sagging skin that are trying to blind me from eyeing my prize at the finish line.

Jesus in me! Beautifully flawless—without a spot, sag, or wrinkle. Through my faith in Jesus Christ, and by the power of the Holy Spirit, I'll be completely perfect eternally in my soul, in my spirit, and in my body.

Live in the Moment

MERCEDES NESFIELD

Your kindness and love will always be with me each day of my life, and I will live forever in your house, Lord.

PSALM 23:6, CEV

When people say, "Age ain't nothing but a number," what do they mean? I've managed to experience eight decades of amazing summers, chilly winters, long brisk walks in the fall, and the renewal of the earth in the spring. Each day that I awaken, I am truly grateful and I know that I've been blessed.

Aging, for me, means knowing God is not finished with my life, and I don't take being alive for granted. I am an only child and I gave birth to only one child. So—I really have never had other siblings to grow up with or compare myself to.

As an only child, you learn to do things on your own and often do them alone. Self-preservation becomes the lens through which you see in order to coexist in the world. Aging for some people is frightening and many become extremely depressed. I believe it's because people love to live in yesterdays instead of embracing the moment.

I live in the moment and stay excited about today and all the opportunities that this body and mind can still take advantage of. I sing in the choir at church, exercise often, feed on the Word of God daily, and let tomorrow take care of itself.

When I look in the mirror, I see a body that has more than eighty years of life's highs and lows. I wouldn't change my journey for the world. My hands have made many mistakes and yet they've done a lot of good over the years. These feet of mine have traveled the globe and I can still dance to a good song. I look at my round stomach that held my most precious gift from God, my baby boy, who is today a beautiful and talented man. The wear and tear on my eyes comes with age, but I can still read my Bible and work a good crossword puzzle, and I praise God for all the things that I have seen and continue to witness. My mouth is the centerpiece of my life. I'm still able to savor tasty foods and good libations, laugh with friends, and speak with a smile to those less fortunate. I have a heart that still holds compassion for others.

So, when people say, "Age ain't nothing but a number," they're right. The aging process is how you choose to embrace life and acknowledge God. Our lives will come to an end at some point and age is not the defining factor. But those of us who believe that Christ our Lord and Savior will return will all be given a new body that will be *ageless*.

LOVE

Reflections ❧ *Love Is a Verb*

Wait on the Lord
JACQUELINE CYRUS-STOUTE, ED.D.

In the Hem of One Garment
CYNTHIA DIAZ

A Woman Who Knows Better Speaks
MONIQUE J. FORTUNÉ

Consider the Quality of Your Materials
REV. MIRIAM MÉNDEZ

Living in the Limelight
KIM MARTIN SADLER

Reflections ❧ *Love Is a Verb*

In John 21, after His resurrection, Jesus posed a question to Peter: "Do you love me?" The disciple readily responded affirmatively. Jesus then asked him again, and again. The multiple questions apparently frustrated Peter, perhaps because it appeared that his love for and loyalty to the Messiah were in doubt. He answered affirmatively each time, yet with every response Peter gave, Jesus followed up with a call to action: "Feed my sheep." Possibly Jesus did not consider words to be a significant demonstration of the kind of love He desired.

Their exchange reminds us that love requires something of us, more than flowery words in greeting cards, or even flowers or gifts. Love requires demonstration. Love requires determination. Love requires action.

Our handicap in the English language is that we have only one word to describe the myriad feelings related to the affection we call love. I can love my home or my new shoes. I can love my job. I can love my sons. I can love my parents. I can love my husband. I can love my best friend. I can love Black people. I can love humanity. Each is love, but each is a type of affection that we have rolled into a not always so neat little ball called love.

We spend millions on Valentine's Day to declare our love with flowers, candy, jewelry, and fancy dinners. We devote holidays to showing love to mothers and fathers and grandparents for the sacrifices they made on our behalf. We even have a day to show our love for Mother Earth. Yes, we talk a lot about love, but we don't necessarily link those feelings of affection to action rooted in love.

But authentic love must translate to action, because feelings are often transitory. We are called to love our children and provide for them even when we despise their actions. In marriage, there are days when we must command that love come from a higher place because our feelings do not currently support us.

Love in action is commanded by the apostle Paul when he calls for mutual submission from husbands and wives. His command for women to submit to their husbands can cause most sisters to chafe. But before putting this condition on women, he admonishes husbands to love their wives as Christ loved the Church—in other words, love your wife enough to die for her. If we considered Paul's words soberly, a lot of us might pause a bit longer before confessing our love.

We do see this love in husbands who stand in harm's way to protect their wives—physically, mentally, emotionally, financially, and even spiritually. Then wives in turn are called to submit to their husbands. *Submit*—the word that bristles against the independent sensibilities of most women today. But I think Paul's admonishment requires at least a second glance before dismissal. I don't think it's a far stretch to say that most sisters would find wifely submission a bit more palatable if they knew that the man to whom this gift was given would lay down his life for her. Submission is a gift that is very fragile, and when it's handled carelessly, it can be irretrievably withdrawn. Many wives have given their husbands this gift, trusting that, above all, he has placed the well-being of his family above his own.

Paul is addressing a delicate balance in marriage that above all commands mutual submission that is extracted from the model of loving submission to Christ. We often see this beautifully expressed in long-term marriages. The wife may refrain from taking her car to the shop because she respects that as the domain of her husband. In turn, her husband does not invite his friends over without first asking her, because the home is her domain. This mutual submission extends beyond so-called traditional roles, like the husband who accepts that his wife is a better money manager and freely hands her his paycheck. Meanwhile, she steps aside when the family wants a fancy meal because he's simply a better cook.

Love is action in marriage and in every human relationship that lays claim to it. We see the love of a mother who would stand in front of a barreling Mack truck to save the life of her child. Love is expressed by the actions of adult children caring for aged parents who no longer even remember their name. Love is demonstrated through caring for the single mother next door by watching her children for an afternoon, just to give her a break. Love is giving to the homeless and giving to the clueless.

We are blessed that we have so many ways to give and receive love. I count myself blessed because I have experienced nearly every form of love possible. I experienced the nurturing love of a caring mother and the protective love of a strong father. I've had the love of a big brother, not quite as protective as Dad's, but watchful over my progress nevertheless.

I've been blessed to experience the romantic love that moves you to plan spending the rest of your life with a man. And then I've known the love at first sight that falls upon the mother of a newborn who has just been introduced to the world. I've felt the love in eyes that look back at you because you are the one entrusted to rear that child to adulthood. I've shared the love of sister-aunts, sister-friends, and sister-mothers in church and in my community. I know the love of and for the Black community. I know the love of and for the beloved community.

I hope that every woman has an opportunity, in her lifetime, to know the many forms and expressions of love that life offers. Most of all, I hope you know the unfailing love of God, which sustains, comforts, and covers you through every step you take in life.

After that, I hope you fully know the love of self. Jesus said in Matthew 22:39 to love God with all that you have in you, but then to "love your neighbor as yourself." Please don't confuse the syntax with the order in which you should love. Jesus expects that you would love yourself, which in turn will allow you to experience love for another, which ripples through the myriad of affections we give to our most desired four-letter word.

Wait on the Lord

JACQUELINE CYRUS-STOUTE, Ed.D.

I was in my fifties, still beautiful, well educated, and a highly respected professional counselor. However, marriage had eluded me. A lonely retirement life stood ahead. My prayer for a husband went unanswered. Yet my faith in God remained steadfast. Most of the men who were interested in me were either married or low-level functionaries. I prayed on.

Just then, Children's Hospital assigned a new dentist to our staff. He was always well dressed, very focused in his work, and professional in his attitude. That was the type I was looking for, but he seemed not to be interested in me. Twice at lunchtime I rode in his car to McDonald's. He was very courteous. He opened and closed the doors for me and also paid the bills.

A couple of years after he was assigned to this office, the federal grant that kept him employed was not renewed, and his office was closed. On his last day on the job, he came over and wished me good-bye. I then gave him my number. For weeks I waited for a call, but none came. Maybe he was not the one for me. Then, one lonely Saturday afternoon he called and invited me to dinner. I accepted the invitation. A series of invitations followed and a close relationship developed.

Now we are both retired and have been happily married for six years. Good things come to those who trust and wait on the Lord.

In the Hem of One Garment

CYNTHIA DIAZ

A woman who had been bleeding for twelve years came up behind Jesus and barely touched His clothes.

MATTHEW 9:20, CEV

 When God created the world, He bequeathed and devised a legacy of love and faith for all of us. God has bequeathed and devised a plan to prosper and not harm us through our DNA (Divinely Necessary Anointing). Today, I am thankful that our Creator has drafted my last will and testament. It has been executed through the wombs and sacred garments of my foremothers. I am the proud beneficiary of the minds, bodies, and spirits of all of the women who touch my life yesterday, today, and tomorrow.

I have proudly worn a bilingual black robe with vibrant multi-color of use and distinction. Colors of pride, justice seeking to be heard, voices crying for a promised land of liberation, and a chorus of "America the Beautiful," "Lift Every Voice and Sing," and "La Borinqueña" can be seen and heard through the many threads that it took to design a customized garment that has been handcrafted by God.

The length of my robe pulsates with the distant sounds of Mother Africa. Its deep pockets have been lined with savory spices from

Puerto Rico and the castaway shores of Cuba. Its distinctive, puffed-up sleeves have been uniquely shaped for arms that have never been too short to reach out to God. Its ample width has been inspired by a joyful journey from my neighboring Justice Sonia Sotomayor housing project benches in the Bronx to a historic first Latina judicial bench bearing my name on Long Island. Its long shiny zipper has allowed me the privilege of stepping in and out of different worlds of knowledge and understanding. Bloodstains of pain were washed from the rear of my wrap, as I intentionally looked forward to the success of my covering. My unseen name on the inside of my cape symbolizes God's visible blessing on the outside of my dressing gown.

My sisters, young and old, Black, brown, and yellow, from many nations, are the witnesses who continue to validate my inheritance. I am the beneficiary of a legacy that has clothed and fed me from housing project benches to benches of higher calling in law and ministry. Countless pots of sunshine-colored rice with savory beans from two islands with one language in common have expanded my personalized Goya waistline with pride.

My road to the Surrogate's Court to claim my fortune has been filled with countless hours of shared joys and many concerns. The will of God was probated without opposition on the day that I surrendered to a higher calling to preach and teach the Gospel of Jesus Christ. My legal robe was stretched beyond the decisions I had written, the judgments I had rendered, and the sentences I had executed, to become my spiritual bequest.

The mantle of God's love that I have inherited can be passed on to future generations. Our individual and joint legacies will be passed on to us the moment we reach out for the hem of His garment.

A Woman Who Knows Better Speaks

MONIQUE J. FORTUNÉ

> For now there are faith, hope, and love. But of these three,
> the greatest is love.
>
> I CORINTHIANS 13:13, CEV

 Sisters. *Hermanas. Mes chéries.* It's time. I do believe I am grown enough to share my voice of experience with confidence. I have been wanting, needing to share this sacred message, what I have learned and am still learning about love and life. This won't take long.

1. Let your temple—body, mind, and spirit—be a dedication to God, the Creator, the source, and the almighty.
2. Let love flow every day by giving positive, intentional service to someone who needs your gifts and talents.
3. Create a blessed space in your home where you can be still and content.
4. Show gratitude for all the past life lessons, no matter how challenging or painful. These life lessons are preparing you for the glorious present and future that is yours to claim.
5. Let your heart be open to pure love in unexpected places and ways.

6. Don't move into a space spiritually, mentally, or physically that does not honor the best of who you are.

7. Make sure you have one or two close friends whom you can speak your deepest truths to.

8. Be gentle with yourself and others.

9. Let a good laugh or a good cry be your soul solace.

10. Give peace, a smile, and a word of encouragement to someone who may come across as hostile or angry—he or she may need your love, smile, and encouragement the most.

11. Cook and/or share a meal with someone you want to get to know better.

12. Give people the gift of sincere listening.

13. Forgive. Forgive again. Forgive yet again. This takes time and work.

14. Spend time in nature. Appreciate the beauty of our world.

15. Let yourself experience the seasons and the full spectrum of love—when it is time to let go, release the experience and/or person with grace and kindness.

Like I said before, I am still learning about love and life. I am a realist. We've got so much happening on this planet that can wound or break the soul. But don't let this world invade the radiance of who you are. Love is still the answer. Just make sure you are asking the right questions.

Consider the Quality of Your Materials

REV. MIRIAM MÉNDEZ

Clothe yourselves with compassion, kindness, humility,
meekness, and patience. Bear with one another and, if anyone
has a complaint against another, forgive each other; just as the
Lord has forgiven you, so you also must forgive. Above all,
clothe yourselves with love, which binds everything together in
perfect harmony.

COLOSSIANS 3:12–14, NIV

If you have ever started a home remodeling
project, you have undoubtedly discovered that
these types of projects take much longer than
you originally thought. Something always goes
wrong. There are hidden repairs you didn't an-
ticipate. And no matter how careful you are in
estimating the cost of labor, materials, and mis-
cellaneous remodeling components, quite often
you go over budget. This is especially true with DIY (do-it-yourself)
projects!

How many trips have you taken to your favorite home improvement store because you realized you measured wrong and cut too
short? Or what about the three-weekend project that turns out to be
unfinished thirty weekends later? Or perhaps in trying to save money
you use cheap material that eventually warp, fall apart, leak, or sim-

ply stop working. Many of us try to cut corners in order to finish the project sooner and have money left over. And usually, all we are left with is an undesirable finished product!

The same is true of marriage. If we consider marriage as a building under construction rather than as a one-day event, we understand that in order to build a strong and stable marriage, we have to consider the quality of the materials we use. With any construction project, if we use cheap materials, we will end up with an unstable end product. In marriage, criticism, impatience, spitefulness, and unfaithfulness are all cheap materials that will weaken your relationship with your spouse and possibly cause the collapse of your marriage.

The apostle Paul gives us the highest-quality materials to use in order to build a strong marriage. Compassion, kindness, humility, meekness, patience, and forgiveness are all solid building blocks that strengthen our relationship with our spouse.

Paul also offers us the most precious material available for a solid marriage. It's not granite, marble, hardwood, bamboo, or composite wood! God's love, the most precious building material of all, must be the foundation of the spouses' love for one another—a love that thinks and includes the other. This love is never halfhearted; rather, it gives fully. It is a love that is strong yet gentle. Godly love is wide enough to accommodate your two personalities and broad enough to embrace and serve others. This kind of love is also high enough to always be in touch with God. This love will last a lifetime, "as long as you both shall live."

It's easy for two imperfect people to succumb to using cheap materials (criticism, impatience, spitefulness, and unfaithfulness) while building their marital bond. The temptation to use inferior materials comes when your spouse does not do what you want or does not act the way you want. But relying on cheap materials will only leave you with an undesirable marriage.

Have you considered the materials you are using to build your marriage lately?

Living in the Limelight

KIM MARTIN SADLER

There is no Holy One like the Lord, no one besides you; there is no Rock like our God.

I SAMUEL 2:2, NRSV

 As a young girl growing up in Harlem, I loved reading books. Books were my best friends, and as you might guess, I developed quite an imagination. As I grew older, I became fond of romantic novels. I dreamed of meeting my future husband in college, so I prayed to God to fulfill the desires of my heart.

I imagined my husband loving me like the sun bringing light to night, needing me like a cool breeze on a hot summer day, and caring for me like rays of the sun on sprouts breaking through soil. I imagined him taking me to exotic places so I could bathe in the muddy Jordan River and cook fish with Balanta women of Guinea-Bissau.

God answered my prayer. I met my loving, caring husband in college. Further, his profession allowed me to travel, experience other cultures, and meet a variety of interesting people. I married a minister.

Going into the marriage, I had no idea what it meant to be a minister's wife. After all, none of the books I had read mentioned ministers, let alone their spouses. More important, God hadn't given me a clue! I grew up in an Episcopal church, where none of the priests were married. Therefore, I had no frame of reference as to expectations or requirements of the clergy's spouse. I especially had no idea what church members wanted, needed, and expected from a "first lady," the title given to ministers' wives in African American churches. Quickly, however, I learned my life would literally be on display—as if I were a mannequin positioned and posed in a brightly lit store window. I would live in a fishbowl where I, alongside my husband, would be loved and ridiculed, adored and vilified. We had become public figures, living in the limelight.

I discovered I would be critiqued on what I wore, how I styled my hair, and with whom I associated. I encountered competition from women who secretly loved my husband and attempted to compete with me for his attention. Like Jesus, my husband would learn how to turn the other cheek, while at other times, he would overturn the tables of the money changers.

Before we married, a highly respected church member approached me and asked, "Do you have a minute?"

"Sure," I said.

"Kim, you are going to be a pastor's wife and your husband has *good* hair. *You* need to do something with yours."

I was stunned—and temporarily speechless. I don't know what hit me the hardest: the reference about *good* hair or her choice of words to let me know she didn't like my *nappy* hair. As dignified as this Harlem girl could get in a tense moment, I let this dear church member know it was none of her business how I styled my hair. Needless to say, she was in shock. To my surprise, though, over time she became my champion and we became close friends. She is no longer with us, but I wish she could see my husband now. He is completely bald and I continue to proudly wear my hair in ethnic styles!

To thrive in my marriage, I recognized that I needed the patience of Sarah, the faith of Hannah, the tenacity of Ruth, and the courage of Esther. These mighty women of the Bible became my spiritual mentors and role models.

A minister's wife—especially one who serves a church largely comprising community leaders—is uniquely positioned. It is not unlike political wives who are always in the limelight—on the arm of their husbands at dinner with the mayor, lunch with the governor, or a holiday party at the White House.

Today, I often return to the Harlem apartment where I grew up. I go to the room where I first opened a book and read. Stories continue to ginger my todays and buoy my tomorrows. And just as it did when I was younger, the lens of my mind begins to see new dreams, imagine the unknown, and pray for possibilities.

LEGACY

Reflections ❦ *Legacy in Action*

Dream Chasers
DAWNN KAREN

Reflections ❧ *Legacy in Action*

I am a civil rights era baby, so I've lived through some exciting periods of our nation's history. The common thread through each pivotal move of history is legacy—what we shall leave behind. What will our lives stand for? I revisit this theme often, because one must live life with purpose and on purpose.

So often, the women who make a difference didn't do what they did in order to attain fame or glory. Certainly, Rosa Parks endured some dark days after she refused to give up her seat on that Montgomery bus on December 1, 1955. She and her husband had to leave the South because she could not find work. Yet, when she died, her body lay in honor in the rotunda of our nation's Capitol. That was never her goal; she just believed it was time for things to change in Montgomery. Leymah Gbowee didn't set out to be a Nobel Prize winner when she led the peace movement in Liberia. She was just sick of the violence and death. In their sacrifices, such women have risen to the forefront and given the rest of us models of womanhood to admire and emulate.

In my personal life and vocation, I stand on the shoulders of great women, who left great legacies: Dr. Dorothy Irene Height, Shirley Chisholm, Barbara Jordan, Margaret Thatcher, and Martha Porcher. I also count among those great women my own grandma, Leona Fisher Starnes Thomas. And my mom, Dorothy C. Johnson, who lived and loved her life with joy and great abundance, as Christ offered, and with great character. They have left this earth but they also left their mark.

That is legacy—when your character, your trademark, your footprint, and your spirit still resonate among the living, and are honored. Someone said character is how you act when you think no one is looking. It's wonderful to have the legacies of great women of character, whom we and others still speak about.

I am always in the midst of women who utter my mom's name, or who try to dress as elegantly as she, and the others whose names I mentioned did, and my soul does a little "happy dance."

Many of us who write in this volume are also at the place in life where we must think about legacy. What shall we leave? Will they speak well of our names? What difference did our lives make while on this earth?

Recently, I hosted Dr. Thelma Davidson Adair, a ninety-five-years-young walking, talking, living legend, who shared with our audience about the importance of living so that the children whom Jesus said, "allow to come unto me," will see legacy in action.

I invite you into this chapter of legacy.

Dream Chasers

DAWNN KAREN

Dear dream chasers,

Some of us forget our dreams because of the constraints of the world—bills, debt, stress, et cetera. We all can recall a place where the pressures of the world did not exist. I think as children we are given the capacity to dream of what we should be when we grow up, but we tend to forget. I discovered that ways to revive the child within include spending time observing children, watching cartoons, and reading children's books. Remember those childhood dreams? With that being said, let's keep dream chasing, kids!

Love, D.K.

Dear dream chasers,

I discovered there are people out there who want you to succeed. Not everyone is conspiring against you. They will help you—find them, accept them, and thank them. Embrace the reality that they may not be in your dream for a lifetime, rather, only for a season. Remember, no man is an island. You were not meant to do this alone. Let's keep dream chasing, kids!

Love, D.K.

Dear dream chasers,

This journey to your dreams entails sacrifice. The revolving door of sacrifice will go around and around. When it stops it will open to sweet victory. Although you sacrifice, realize that you are not the only one who has pushed through this revolving door. There are others who have gone through it as well. Won't you ask them to slow down the revolving door before it stops to open to your sweet victory? For you must "ask, and it shall be given you; seek, and ye shall find; knock, and it shall be opened unto you" (Matthew 7:7, KJV). There is humility in asking for help from others. Let's push pride aside by reaching out for help to slow down the revolving door. It is almost opening out to your sweet pathway to victory. Let's keep dream chasing, kids!

Love, D.K.

Dear dream chasers,

In your quest for your dreams there are people who will empower you and disempower you. If you speak to a particular person and he or she continually helps you brainstorm—that is empowerment. If you speak to a particular person and he or she unceasingly badgers you about what you should be doing—that is disempowerment. Please note most people are unaware of how they can empower or disempower you and your aspirations. Choose to share your vision often with those who empower you and seldom with those who disempower you. Be kind to them and, most important, to yourself. Remember it is imperative that you keep your spirits high in the pursuit of your dreams.

Let's keep dream chasing, kids!

Love, D.K.

On my last stop as Ambassador-at-Large for International Religious Freedom, I insisted on going to Liberia, a nation that already had experienced a coup. I met with a number of women who had been injured or violated during the war. Many had been raped or violated in other horrible ways that rendered them unable to perform sexually. And because they could not function sexually, they had been cast out of their villages. As a result, these women carried both physical and emotional pain. They needed healing.

But what I found impressive is that even amid these atrocities, the women of Liberia had come together in an unparalleled demonstration of sisterhood and changed the course of a nation in peril. Their children were dying in war, and the mothers had grown weary of death and funerals. They put aside all differences and united around a single issue: The war must end.

Ironically, the war was rooted in issues of religious and ethnic strife. Nevertheless, Muslim and Christian women united across Liberia in their resolve to stop the fighting and the killing of their children. At first, they united in a form of passive resistance. They refused to sleep with their men until something was done about the war. As they mounted their resistance, the women held hands and got to know each other. The Muslim and Christian women took bold steps and attended the funerals of the other faith. Eventually, they made a human chain all the way to their Parliament and President Charles Taylor. They refused to go home until the war ended.

The women, Muslim and Christian alike, captivated a nation. All dressed in white to symbolize peace, they declared, "Our faith is going to stop this." They also insisted that women become a part of Parliament and the decision-making process of their nation, and they demanded that the men who were not a part of making peace be put out of negotiations.

One sister, Leymah Gbowee, was a pivotal force in the women's movement, and her story is beautifully recalled in a moving documentary titled *Pray the Devil Back to Hell*. The title was taken from a statement Gbowee had made about President Taylor and the Liberian rebels. Both sides claimed to be religious. The rebels professed to be loyal Muslims, while President Taylor claimed to be a devout Christian who could "pray the devil out of hell." Gbowee and the other women determined that it had become the women's responsibility in this interfaith coalition to pray the devil (of war) right back to hell.

Gbowee was later awarded a Nobel Prize for leading the women's peace movement that helped bring an end to the Second Liberian Civil War in 2003. Through her leadership, thousands of women staged pray-ins and nonviolent protests demanding reconciliation and the resuscitation of high-level peace talks. The pressure pushed President Taylor into exile. Gbowee's efforts, along with those of collaborator Ellen Johnson Sirleaf, ushered in a period of peace and enabled a free presidential election in 2005, which Sirleaf won. With her victory, Liberia became the first African nation to have a female president.

Gbowee, Sirleaf, and Tawakkol Karman were awarded the 2011 Nobel Peace Prize "for their non-violent struggle for the safety of women and for women's rights to full participation in peace-building work."

I believe all women can learn from the story of the Liberian women and how they became a political force against violence and against their government. But there have been other movements by women that have changed nations and attitudes. Candy Lightner founded MADD (Mothers Against Drunk Driving) in 1980, after her daughter was killed by a repeat DUI offender. She was joined by other mothers who had lost children to the same fate. Since its inception, MADD has been a powerful force impacting legislation and public opinion regarding driving while intoxicated.

Women banded together during the suffrage movement to gain the right to vote. They marched with their babies in tow because they were determined their time had come.

Collectively and individually, women of every color have been agents of change. Historian Laurel Thatcher Ulrich said, "Well behaved women rarely make history." I thank God for the sisters throughout history who have been willing to risk society's label of "behaving badly" to bring much-needed change to the course of humanity.

Aung San Suu Kyi—This Burmese opposition politician who advocated for women's rights once stated, "In societies where men are truly confident of their own worth, women are not merely tolerated but valued."

Benazir Bhutto—The eleventh Prime Minister of Pakistan, Bhutto was the first woman to head a Muslim state. During her leadership, she ended military dictatorship in her country and fought for women's rights. She was assassinated in a suicide attack in 2007.

Michelle Obama—The first African American first lady of the United States, Obama was raised in a one-bedroom Chicago apartment before she went on to excel in academics at Princeton and Harvard.

Oprah Winfrey—The African American former talk show host turned cable network station owner is a generous philanthropist born to a poor single mother in Mississippi, and today is worth $2.7 billion.

Rosa Parks—Also known as the "First Lady of Civil Rights," Parks became a pioneer of civil rights in a racially segregated Alabama in the 1950s when she refused to give away her seat in the "colored" section to a white passenger on a bus in Montgomery. Her act of defiance sparked the Montgomery bus boycott that crippled the state capital's public transport system.

Indira Gandhi—She served India as prime minister for fifteen years, paving the way for democracy in India until her assassination in 1984.

Fannie Lou Hamer—A Black American voting rights activist, civil rights leader, and philanthropist, Hamer was instrumental in organizing Mississippi's Freedom Summer for the Student Nonviolent Coordinating Committee. She is credited with the phrase, "I'm sick and tired of being sick and tired."

Shirley Chisholm—After her election as first African American U.S. congresswoman in 1968, Chisholm became the first major party Black candidate to make a bid for the U.S. presidency, in 1972.

Sojourner Truth—An abolitionist and women's rights activist, Truth was born into slavery in Ulster County, New York, but escaped with her infant daughter to freedom in 1826. She is still lauded for her speech, "Ain't I a Woman?"

Coretta Scott King—A Black American civil rights and human rights activist, King was the wife of slain civil rights leader Martin Luther King Jr.

Harriet Tubman—A former slave, Tubman was a famous conductor of the Underground Railroad. During a ten-year span, she made nineteen trips into the South and escorted more than three hundred slaves to freedom. She once proudly pointed out to abolitionist Frederick Douglass that in all of her journeys she had never lost a single passenger.

Mary McLeod Bethune—This extraordinary educator, civil rights leader, and government official founded the National Council of Negro Women. She also founded Bethune-Cookman College—with her faith and less than $1.50.

Dorothy Irene Height—The godmother of the civil rights movement, Height spent her life fighting for civil rights and women's rights.

Sadie Tanner Mossell Alexander—The first Black woman to earn a Ph.D. in the United States, Alexander was also the was the first woman to receive a law degree from the University of Pennsylvania Law School and was the first national president of Delta Sigma Theta Sorority, Inc.

Wangari Maathai—The Kenyan-born environmentalist, pro-democracy activist, women's rights campaigner, and founder of the Green Belt Movement was awarded the Nobel Peace Prize for efforts to prevent conflict through protection of scarce resources.

Malala Yousafzai—This Pakistani schoolgirl defied threats from the Taliban to campaign for the right to education. She survived being shot in the head by the Taliban and has become a global advocate for women's rights, especially the right to attend school.

Claribel Alegría—A Nicaraguan novelist with more than twenty-five published works, Alegría is a powerful voice in contemporary literature in Central America. The George Washington University grad focused on the people's movement, which helped overthrow dictator Anastasio Somoza Debayle.

Hilda Lucia Solis—A member of the Los Angeles County Board of Supervisors for District 1, Solis previously served as the twenty-fifth United States Secretary of Labor from 2009 to 2013, as part of the administration of President Barack Obama. She is a member of the Democratic Party and served in the United States House of Representatives from 2001 to 2009, representing the 31st and 32nd congressional districts of California, which include East Los Angeles and the San Gabriel Valley.

Sonia Sotomayor—Being the third female justice and the first Latina to sit on the bench of the Supreme Court of the United States is no small accomplishment for the New York City native. In addition to her inspirational work as a Latina in the legal world, Sotomayor published her memoir, *My Beloved World*, in 2013, which recounts her early life growing up in housing projects in New York and the challenges she overcame.

Dolores Huerta—Along with Cesar Chavez, Huerta cofounded the National Farm Workers Association, which eventually became the United Farm Workers (UFW), in order to bring farmers together in a union that fights to protect their rights. She is a labor leader and civil rights activist who has also advocated for immigrants' and women's rights, earning her the Eleanor Roosevelt Award for Human Rights and the Presidential Medal of Freedom.

Rigoberta Menchú Tum—She is an activist who has dedicated her life to helping the world recognize the plight of Guatemala's indigenous peoples during and after the Guatemalan civil war. She has promoted indigenous rights in the country, ran for President of Guatemala in 2007 and 2011, and even received the Nobel Peace Prize in 1992 and the Princess of Asturias Award in 1998. Her fight for the people of Guatemala has forever inspired recognition of indigenous rights in South America.

Vilma Martinez—The Mexican American civil rights attorney was the first woman appointed to serve as the U.S. ambassador to Argentina. She was appointed by President Barack Obama in 2009 but has been a diplomat since President Jimmy Carter appointed her to her first position in the U.S. diplomatic corps in 1977.

Linda Chavez-Thompson—A Mexican American union leader and former vice president of the American Federation of Labor and Congress of Industrial Organizations (1995–2007), Chavez-Thomson works on behalf of the fifty-six national and international unions to represent more than eleven million workers.

Cristina Fernández de Kirchner—Argentina's first elected female president, Kirchner took office in 2007 and was reelected in 2011. Previously, she served as first lady under former president Nestor Kirchner, as a national deputy, and as a national senator for three terms.

Michelle Bachelet—The first female president of Chile, Bachelet served from 2006 to 2010, and has since been appointed as the head of UN Women.

Dilma Rousseff—President of Brazil since 2011 and the first woman to hold the office, Rousseff previously served as the chief of staff to President Luiz Inácio Lula da Silva. Her distinguished honors include receiving the Woodrow Wilson Public Service Award and being named one of Forbes's most powerful women in the world.

Soledad O'Brien—The Cuban American is recognized as one of the top journalists who fight for social change. She has won an Emmy award for cohosting *The Know Zone* and a Goodermote Humanitarian Award for her reporting on Hurricane Katrina and the 2004 Indian Ocean tsunami.

Concepcion Picciotto—Commonly known as Conchita, Picciotto has been living in Lafayette Square in Washington, D.C., since August 1, 1981, when she set up a peace camp across from the White House in order to protest nuclear arms. She is known for carrying out the longest continuous act of political protest in the U.S. and was featured in Michael Moore's 2004 documentary, *Fahrenheit 9/11*.

Alicia Dickerson Montemayor—This Mexican American activist crossed many barriers for women. As vice president general of the League of United Latin American Citizens, she was the first woman elected to a national office that wasn't created specifically for a woman. She encouraged girls and women to join the Latin American activism movement and was designated as a women's history honoree by the National Women's History Project.

Jovita Idár—A Mexican American journalist, Idár was a major figure who worked to advance the civil rights of Mexican Americans. She wrote for *La Crónica* newspaper under a pseudonym, exposing the poor living conditions of Mexican American workers, and supported the Mexican revolution in 1910. She was the first president of the League of Mexican Women, founded in 1911 to offer free education to Mexican children in Laredo, Texas.

The Mirabal Sisters—commonly known as Patrisia, Dede, Minerva, and Maria Teresa, the four sisters became involved in the political movement against dictator Trujillo. They formed the 14th of June movement in order to oppose his regime, but they were incarcerated and tortured on several occasions, resulting in death for three of the sisters (Patrisia was 36, Maria was 34, and Antonia was 25). The day of their deaths, November 25, is now officially the International Day for the Elimination of Violence Against Women.

Claudia de la Cruz—As the founder of Da Urban Butterflies (DUB), Cruz is dedicated to youth outreach for Latinas in the Washington Heights area of New York City. The group helps empower young women between the ages of eighteen and thirty with sex education and career workshops.

Ellen Ochoa—The first Latina astronaut, Ochoa is also the coinventor of three patents related to optical inspection systems. She received her doctorate in electrical engineering from Stanford University and is currently the director of the Johnson Space Center.

Mary Church Terrell—A writer and civil rights and women's rights activist, Terrell was the first president of the National Association of Colored Women and the first Black woman to represent the U.S. Congress of Women. Her father was one of the wealthiest men in the South, yet she devoted herself to service. She also was the first Black woman to serve on the Washington, D.C., Board of Education.

Betty Shabazz—A civil rights activist and the wife of slain civil rights leader Malcolm X, Shabazz was a director of the Medgar Evers College Office of Communications and Public Relations.

Daisy Bates—A civil rights activist, Bates was the principal adviser to the Little Rock Nine as they strived to integrate Little Rock Central High School. Along with her husband, she published a newspaper that kept African Americans abreast of events.

Nannie Helen Burroughs—One of the founders of National Association of Colored Women, Burroughs also founded the National Training School for Women and Girls, in Washington, D.C., and was an associate editor of the *Christian Banner*. She was a prolific writer and orator as well as a civil rights activist.

Ida B. Wells—This prolific African American journalist was also a suffragist, sociologist, and early civil rights movement leader.

Wilma Mankiller—This activist and political leader was the first female principal chief of the Cherokee Nation and was awarded the Presidential Medal of Freedom. Mankiller became politically active in the 1960s as an advocate for American Indian people. She joined Indians of All Tribes (IAT), a group of eighty to ninety mostly Indian college students who occupied Alcatraz Island to demand "the return of Alcatraz to Native American Indians and sufficient funding to build, maintain, and operate an Indian cultural complex and a university."

LaDonna Harris—An activist and the founder/president of Americans for Indian Opportunity, a global organization for the economic, political, and cultural rights of indigenous peoples, Harris received appointments during five U.S. presidential administrations.

Sacagawea—An explorer and interpreter whose knowledge ensured the success of the Lewis and Clark expedition, she was given the title of Honorary Sergeant, Regular Army in 2001.

Cassandra Manuelito-Kerkvliet—When she was named president of Antioch University, Manuelito-Kerkvliet became the first American Indian woman president of a mainstream university. (About half of the nation's tribal colleges are led by Native women presidents.)

Cecilia Fire Thunder—The Oglala Lakota tribe's first woman president, Fire Thunder has fought against domestic abuse, asserting that it is not a part of traditional culture. She has also been a leader for women's reproductive rights.

Anna Mae Aquash (Mi'kmaq name Naguset Eask)—An activist from Nova Scotia, Canada, Aquash became a member of the American Indian Movement and participated in the 1972 Trail of Broken Treaties and occupation of the U.S. Department of the Interior headquarters in Washington, D.C., as well as the Wounded Knee Incident in 1973. In February 1976, her body was found on the Pine Ridge Indian reservation in South Dakota. She was initially determined to have died from exposure but was later found to have been murdered by an execution-style gunshot.

Buffalo Calf Road Woman, or **Brave Woman**—This Northern Cheyenne woman saved her wounded warrior brother, Chief Comes in Sight, in the Battle of the Rosebud in 1876. Her rescue helped rally the Cheyenne warriors to win the battle. She fought side-by-side with her husband in the Battle of the Little Bighorn that same year. In 2005 Northern Cheyenne storytellers broke more than one hundred years of silence about the battle, crediting Buffalo Calf Road Woman with striking the blow that knocked Lieutenant Colonel George Armstrong Custer. Later, from that strike, he died.

Elouise Pepion Cobell, Yellow Bird Woman—An elder and activist, banker, rancher, and Native American leader, Cobell was the lead plaintiff in the groundbreaking litigation *Cobell v. Salazar*, which challenged the United States' mismanagement of trust funds belonging to more than five hundred thousand Native American individuals. In 2010 the government approved a $3.4 billion settlement for the trust case.

Eliza Burton "Lyda" Conley—An American lawyer of Native American and European descent, Conley was the first woman admitted to the Kansas bar. In 1909 she was the first Native American woman admitted to argue a case before the Supreme Court of the United States. Her case is believed to have been one in which "a plaintiff argued that the burying grounds of Native Americans were entitled to federal protection." (Per wikipedia article.)

Dahteste—A wife and mother who took part in raiding parties with her first husband, Ahnandia, Dahteste was a compatriot of Geronimo and companion of Lozen on many raids. She was fluent in English and acted as a messenger and translator for the Apache. She also became a mediator and trusted scout at times for the U.S. Cavalry and was instrumental in negotiating Geronimo's surrender.

Suzan Shown Harjo—An advocate for American Indian rights, poet, writer, lecturer, curator, and policy advocate, Harjo has helped Native peoples recover more than one million acres. She served as congressional liaison for Indian affairs in the Carter administration and later as president of the National Council of American Indians.

Mary Musgrove—A colonial American interpreter and negotiator of mixed Yamacraw and English ancestry, Musgrove helped facilitate the development of colonial Georgia and became an important intermediary between Muscogee Creek Indians and the English colonists.

Ingrid Washinawatok El-Issa—An internationally known member of the Menominee Nation of upper Wisconsin, El-Issa was murdered by guerrillas in Colombia in 1999. She was the chair of the NGO Committee on the United Nations International Decade of the World's Indigenous Peoples, a delegate to the United Nations Commission on Human Rights, an NGO representative in consultative status to the UN for the International Indian Treaty Council, and a member of the UN Working Group on Indigenous Populations.

Charmaine White Face, or **Zumila Wobaga**—Known for her work in support of Native American rights, Wobaga is the coordinator of the Defenders of the Black Hills, a volunteer organization centered on efforts to encourage the United States government to honor the Fort Laramie Treaties of 1851 and 1868.

Sarah Winnemucca—A prominent female Paiute activist and educator, Winnemucca helped secure the release of her people from the Yakima reservation after the Bannock War of 1878. She was an influential figure in the development of the United States' nineteenth-century Indian policies.

The heartfelt experiences shared in *Soul Sisters* demonstrate the strength of women, both singly and collectively. The movements we have spawned are proof of our strength and our fortitude. It is that determination that moved the women to continue marching toward Jesus's tomb, although they did not know how they would roll away the stone, even as the men were in hiding, not wanting to meet the same fate as their teacher. The strength of a woman moved Harriet Tubman to risk her life and venture into the South more than a dozen times to free more than three hundred slaves.

I sincerely hope you find that same strength within yourself, the might of Soul Sisters who have answered life's call at every turn with, "Here am I; send me."

ABOUT THE AUTHOR

 Ambassador Suzan Johnson Cook—"Ambassador Sujay," as she is affectionately called—was the former U.S. 3rd Ambassador-at-Large for International Religious Freedom during the Obama administration. She made twenty-eight diplomatic stops abroad in twenty months. Always drawn to the female leaders around the globe, she engaged women leaders wherever she went.

A native New Yorker, she resides in Harlem and Washington, D.C., currently serving as a distinguished visiting fellow at the Catholic University of America. She also owns and operates Charisma Speakers/Cook Global Communications and builds the ProVoice movement for women.

An author of twelve books, Cook is a prolific writer and speaker, and whether in writing or speaking, she hopes her words bring hope, healing, and restoration. Her monthly gatherings for women can be found at ProVoiceMovementforWomen.com, and her annual retreats for women leaders can be found at WomenOntheWorldstage.com.

For speaking requests or to book or hire a speaker, please visit CharismaSpeakers.com.

Her other titles with Tarcher/Penguin, such as *Becoming a Woman of Destiny: Turning Life's Trials into Triumphs*, can be found in hardback or paperback, in bookstores or online.

ABOUT THE CONTRIBUTORS

JETOLA ANDERSON-BLAIR
Jetola is a human resources consultant and entrepreneur hailing from Jamaica. She is also a wife, mother, writer, and marathoner living in Houston, Texas. She's the author of *In My Sister's Shoes* (Cross Keys Press, 1999) and a proud member of Delta Sigma Theta Sorority, Inc., and Jack and Jill of America. She attends Friendship Community Bible Church in Sugar Land, Texas, where she serves as a cheerful usher.

REV. DIONNE P. BOISSIÈRE, M.DIV.
Dionne, associate minister at New Hope Baptist Church in Danbury, Connecticut, is a proud Caribbean American and the first woman of African descent to serve as chaplain of the Church Center for the United Nations (CCUN). Her vocational experience includes corporate training; organizational development; socioeconomic, religious, and community improvement programming; women's religious studies; church stewardship; liturgy; and worship. She is featured among the so-called "next generation" of Black women ministers and published in *Those Preaching Women: A Multicultural Collection* (Judson Press, 2008). She also received her master of divinity from Union Theological Seminary in New York, and is currently pursuing doctoral studies to continue work focused on bridging the gap between the church, academy, and society.

CHERÉ BROWN

Cheré Brown, LCSW (and approved alcohol and drug supervisor), is the daughter of Reverend Dr. William H. Graham and the late Reverend Dr. Eleanor Graham Bryant. A third-generation social worker and a licensed psychotherapist and consultant practicing in Baltimore, she is also a lay leader at Empowerment Temple African Methodist Episcopal Church. She is a proud African American mother of two brilliant sons, one special daughter-in-law, and one amazing grandson.

M. GASBY BROWN

Gasby believes in the power of praise and prayer. She has a joyous testimony about the goodness and grace of Jesus Christ and is a respected philanthropic expert, helping nonprofit organizations across the country to strengthen their fund-raising. Gasby is also a prolific visual artist, capturing the richness of her proud African American heritage and experiences through her art. Her professional career has included positions as New York correspondent for BET, reporter for Fox 5 (WNYW) in New York, financial correspondent for the *McCreary Report*, and host of "Black Viewpoint," a news segment on WNYC. Gasby is also the author of *Art of Praise*.

TERI COAXUM

Teri is a mother, author, blogger, motivational speaker, professor, and community leader, currently serving as the U. S. Small Business Administration Office of Advocacy Region II advocate, covering the states of New York and New Jersey, as well as the U.S. Virgin Islands and the commonwealth of Puerto Rico. Prior to her appointment, Teri's roles included serving as the first African American woman deputy state director for Senator Charles Schumer and administrative manager in the Kings County District Attorney's office. Both roles allowed her to work closely with government and local officials, advocate for underserved communities, and empower through economic stability, job readiness, and technological advancement. She is a graduate of John Jay College of Criminal Justice, the Metropolitan College of New York paralegal program, the Harvard University executive program, the Annette Strauss Institute for Civic Life executive training program, and Coro New York Leadership Center.

DR. CARETHA FRANKS CRAWFORD
Caretha, a native of North Carolina, is proud to be an African American. She is founder of the Gateway to Wholeness Church Ministries in Largo, Maryland, and In Pursuit of His Presence Worship Arts Ministries in Maryland and North Carolina. She is the host of CarethaTV, an Internet television channel, and author of *Dance, God's Gift to You* (Xulon Press, 2010) and *Hold On to Your Dream* (Creation House, 2014). Dr. Crawford also produces handcrafted greeting cards under the label Kingdom Greetings 4U®. She is a gifted speaker and entrepreneur whose business endeavors are chronicled at carethacrawford.com. She lives in Mitchellville, Maryland, with her husband, Pastor Clarence Crawford.

JACQUELINE CYRUS-STOUTE, ED.D.
Jacqueline is a proud African American who retired from the District of Columbia Public Schools in 2007 with thirty-three years of service. As a teacher and professional counselor, she developed effective individualized education plans and positive behavior support plans. Additionally, she has more than fifteen years of private-practice experience as a licensed professional counselor. Her case management and counseling experiences have enabled her to acquire unique skills that are transferable to community mental health program settings.

THELMA DAY, ED.D.
Thelma is a prominent leadership development consultant. She is the dean of academic affairs at Los Angeles City College. Pepperdine University awarded her a doctor of education degree in institutional

management. Thelma is a member of numerous organizations, including Delta Sigma Theta Sorority, Inc., and the Links, Incorporated. She resides in Los Angeles with her husband and their two daughters.

TERESA DELGADO, PH.D.

Teresa is director of peace and justice studies and associate professor of religion and ethics at Iona College in New Rochelle, New York. She received her doctorate from Union Theological Seminary, coedited *Augustine and Social Justice* (Rowman and Littlefield, 2015), and has published numerous articles and book chapters, including "Good Teaching Is Like Good Sex," in *Teaching Theology and Religion* (Wabash, 2015); "Beyond Procreativity: Heterosexuals Queering Marriage," in *Queer Christianities: Lived Religion in Transgressive Forms* (New York University Press, 2014); and "Dead in the Water . . . Again," in *Theological Perspectives for Life, Liberty, and the Pursuit of Happiness: Public Intellectuals for the Twenty-first Century* (Palgrave Macmillan, 2013). She is currently writing a book titled *Loving Sex: Envisioning a Relevant Catholic Sexual Ethic*, through a grant from the Louisville Institute. Teresa serves as president of the board of directors for WESPAC Foundation (Westchester Peace Action Coalition) and lives in Mount Vernon, New York, with her husband and their four children.

CYNTHIA DIAZ, J.D., D.MIN.

Cynthia is a Bronx-born Cuban–Puerto Rican who married at age twenty, raised five children, attended Hofstra University Law School, and built a highly successful law practice over a period of fourteen years. She was the first female special prosecutor and Latina associate justice of the Hempstead Village Court. As a master of divinity and doctor of ministry graduate of New York Theological Seminary, she served as the director of student affairs, vocational discernment, and the women's center. At present, she is passionately serving on the ministerial team of the Congregational Church of South Hempstead,

United Church of Christ, while also practicing as an "up and running legal and spiritual advocate" in a mobile office that meets the needs of her clients in their places of need and healing. Her personal and professional experiences have been filled with dreams to give birth to the literary seeds that have been growing inside her.

DR. RAMONA HOAGE EDELIN

Ramona is a scholar, activist, and executive consultant with forty years of experience in leadership to uplift and advance African Americans and the economically disadvantaged. She has served as executive director of the District of Columbia Association of Chartered Public Schools since 2006. A nationally respected lecturer, she has given media presentations on network, public, and cable television and radio, as well as in print and other published venues. Third World Press has recently published her book, *We the Village Achieving Our Collective Greatness Now*.

LaTONYA ELLIS

LaTonya is a graduate of Middle Tennessee State University in Murfreesboro, and an active member of Delta Sigma Theta Sorority, Inc., Nashville Alumnae Chapter. She is employed as a communications manager for a trade association. Most important, she is the mother of two sons, one of whom was senselessly murdered in 2012 at age seventeen. She relies on her strong faith to give her hope for her other son and for other African American males, so that they do not meet the same fate. LaTonya resides in Nashville, Tennessee, with her youngest son, Caleb.

MONIQUE J. FORTUNÉ

Monique is a native New Yorker celebrating her African/Haitian/St. Kitts–Nevis ancestral roots as a servant leader and collaborator, educator, poet, writer, and media consultant. She currently teaches the first-year experience course at Bronx Community College. She is also president of Fortuné and Associates, a consulting company specializing in public speaking and media and business communication strategies, serving such clients as the famed Apollo Theater in Harlem, Hudson River Museum, Mentoring in Medicine, and WFUV-FM, Fordham University's public radio station. In addition, Monique teaches communication, mass media theory, and organizational communication courses at Fordham University. Before establishing Fortuné and Associates, she was promotions director at New York City radio station WWRL-AM, and development and marketing director at WFUV-FM. She also served as radio curator for the Museum of Television and Radio, now known as the Paley Center for Media. Monique feels particularly blessed to have supportive family and friends. But most of all, she gives God all honor and glory for every day she has the opportunity to live, love, laugh, and serve.

DR. NATALIE A. FRANCISCO

Natalie received bachelor and master of arts degrees in Christian education from International Bible College in Independence, Missouri, and a doctorate in Christian education from Carolina University of Theology. She has served as co-pastor of Calvary Community Church (C3) and cofounder of Calvary Christian Academy in Hampton, Virginia, alongside her husband, Bishop L. W. Francisco III. She is currently campus pastor of C3 Atlanta, located in College Park, Georgia. Natalie has also served extensively in full-time ministry for more than twenty-nine years in areas of leadership in both the music and arts and Christian education departments of her local church. As founder and executive director of the Women of Worth Conference and the Women of Worth and Worship Institute (WOWWI), Natalie seeks to provide godly and practical instruction to women who desire to learn and implement biblical truths and principles from her life's lessons. As a personal mentor and a consultant, she strives to equip others to excel in the areas of ministry, daily living, and education through her four books, conferences, seminars, and retreats.

GWEN FRANKLIN

Gwen began her career in radio at Howard University's WHUR-FM, while earning her bachelor of arts in communications (radio/TV and film). She received her master of business administration degree from Baruch College/City University of New York. In 1996, Gwen founded B. Lifted Up!, a business and financial consulting firm with a mission of "Empowerment Through Insight, Education and Training." B. Lifted Up! has provided its consulting services to Bloomberg Radio, colleges and universities, churches, community development corporations, and private industry. Gwen resides in Teaneck, New Jersey, and is the proud mother of Kahlil X. Daniel, a gifted performing artist, Howard University graduate, and a force of unlimited potential in the universe.

LITA GAITHERS

Lita is an African American singer/songwriter, a playwright, and co-author of the Broadway musical *It Ain't Nothin' but the Blues*, which was nominated for four Tony Awards, including Best Musical of 1999. Lita's latest gospel EP, *In the Beauty of Holiness/The Naomi Project*, is available on iTunes. She is a member of West Angeles Church of God in Christ in Los Angeles and has been married to Elder Oscar Owens Jr. for thirty years.

DEBRA GAUSE

Debra resides in Brooklyn, New York, and is an employee of the Board of Education Food Services. She is cofounder of Tradition, an organization that helps seniors. She is a graduate of Cornell University's Union women's studies program and attended Hunter College, majoring in child psychology.

ROXANNE M. GIRARD-NESFIELD

Roxanne is a Japanese American, second-generation Nisei. She is a principal of Ito and Girard Associates and owner of Neighborhood Real Estate, a real estate development company that focuses on building affordable homes and devotes time to many nonprofit organizations in their community. She resides in San Diego, California, with her husband and family of friends.

CAMILLE M. HENDERSON

Camille is a native of Newark, Delaware, and is a proud African American. She is a recent graduate of Spelman College, where she received a bachelor of arts degree in political science. While at Spelman, Camille served as senior intern for the Bonner Scholars Program, as well as lead chapel assistant for Sisters Chapel. She was also selected as a fellow for the Spelman College social justice program, in which she conducted research on the role of religion in the mitigation of sex trafficking within the United States. Camille is continuing her research as a Robert W. Woodruff Fellow at Candler School of Theology, Emory University, where she will obtain a master of divinity.

KIM A. HILL

Kim is a native of New York, born in Harlem. She earned two master's degrees at the former C.W. Post campus of Long Island University in the areas of special education and school administration. Kim is a dedicated educator, serving her community as an elementary school principal in Jamaica, Queens, New York. She passionately supervises one of the largest New York City public schools in Queens, with more than fifteen hundred students. She is proud to provide an outstanding learning community to students whose cultural heritage represents six of the seven continents. Kim has always exemplified a passion for her community and sisterhood, as she is a proud member of the St. Albans Chamber of Commerce, Alpha Kappa Alpha Sorority, Inc., and the ProVoice movement.

CHAPLAIN VIRGINIA JACKSON

Virginia, a proud African American, was the first woman chief of chaplain service at the Department of Veterans Affairs, Palo Alto Health

Care System. She received a master of divinity from the American Baptist Seminary of the West in California, and earned a doctor of ministry degree from San Francisco Theological Seminary. She was ordained by the American Baptist Churches USA denomination in 1996. In addition to performing pastoral tasks, she directs the Menlo Park In-patient Chorus, and has served as a panel member on the Institutional Review Board (IRB) of Medical Research on Human Subjects at Stanford University Hospital. Virginia has been assistant pastor of First Baptist Church in Menlo Park, California, associate pastor of Crosswalk Community Church in Sunnyvale, California, and pastor of Christian education at Saint Matthews Episcopal Church in San Mateo, California. In 2010, she received the Outstanding Service Award and was named Chaplain of the Year by the Department of Veterans Affairs National Black Chaplains Association Inc. In 2012 she celebrated her seventieth birthday with a skydive from twelve thousand feet.

AVIS JONES-DeWEEVER, PH.D.

Avis is an Exceptional Leadership Strategist, diversity expert, and founder of the Exceptional Leadership Institute for Women. She recently served as the youngest top executive officer of a major national membership organization, reaching four million women in the U.S. and around the world. Today, her coaching, courses, workshops, and events help women executives and entrepreneurs move further and faster in their careers while building a home life that they love. Those who wish to join the sisterhood of women committed to creating the career and life they've always imagined can visit exceptionalleadershipinstitute.com.

DAWNN KAREN

Dawnn, B.A., M.A., is a New York City–based fashion psychologist and founder of the fashion psychology field. She holds a master of arts degree from Columbia University's counseling psychology program and is a former model, fashion public relations representative, and designer. She specializes in "styling from the inside out by bridging the gap between perception and reality." Dawnn has worked with clients all over the world, written for several international publications, performed many speaking engagements, and contributed as an international media expert. Her public speaking focus is to disseminate her Dream Chasers initiatives through her field of fashion psychology.

DR. CHERYL KIRK-DUGGAN

Cheryl is a professor of religion at Shaw University Divinity School in Raleigh, North Carolina, and an ordained elder in full connection in the Christian Methodist Episcopal (CME) Church. A loving African American, she has written more than twenty books and numerous articles and book chapters. She has two undergraduate degrees in music, a master of music, a master of divinity, and a doctor of philosophy in religion, from Baylor University. She has memberships in numerous professional societies and is a former CME denominational representative to the General Assembly of the National Council of Churches. Cheryl is featured in Malka Drucker's *White Fire: A Portrait of Women Spiritual Leaders in America* (Skylight Paths, 2003). The recipient of many awards of leadership, empowerment, excellence, and mentoring, Cheryl is an avid athlete who completed her first full marathon in 2010 and enjoys hot yoga. She also quilts occasionally, and is a musician who loves to tinker with her flowers. She appreciates family and friends, and embraces laughter as her best medicine on the quest for a healthy, holistic, spiritual life.

RONNEAK M. LEE

Ronneak was born and raised in Rankin, Pennsylvania, a suburb of Pittsburgh. She is a licensed minister serving at First Corinthian Baptist Church in Harlem. She is the creator of Beloved, Beautiful and No Longer Bound Ministry. Ronneak will graduate with the master of arts in pastoral care and counseling program from New York Theological Seminary.

REVEREND JUDY MALANA

Judy is an ordained minister with the General Council of the Assemblies of God. She currently serves as an active duty navy chaplain and is the first Asian American female to do so. She is inspired every day by the beautiful and courageous women God has put in her path. Judy is married to Mark Clester, with whom she has four incredible children: Jonah, Joshua, Jeremiah, and Jordan. She is also the sister of a phenomenal woman, Jerri Malana, whose passion and tenacious spirit encourages others to pursue their deepest dreams.

REVEREND EYESHA K. MARABLE

Reverend Eye, as she is affectionately known by many, holds a bachelor of arts degree in journalism and Spanish, a master of science degree in nonprofit management, postgraduate certification in organizational development, and a master of divinity degree from Drew Theological School. She is an itinerate elder and coordinator of liturgical dance, First Episcopal District, African Methodist Episcopal Church. Rev. Eye is founding director of the National Liturgical Dance Network (natldancenetwork.com). She is proud to be an African American mother of Judah and Honor, and wife of Edward B. Marable Jr., Esq., former councilman in Orange, New Jersey.

LUCIA K. McBATH

Lucia is the mother of Jordan Russell Davis, who at the tender age of seventeen was murdered by a middle-aged man who was agitated about how loud Jordan and his friends were playing music in their car. Currently she is championing and fighting for commonsense gun legislation and solutions to the issue of our country's rampant gun violence. Lucia is a national spokesperson for Everytown for Gun Safety/Moms Demand Action for Gun Sense in America and acts as faith and community outreach organizer. In her work as a gun safety advocate, she has testified before the U.S. Senate Judiciary Committee, the Subcommittee on the "Stand Your Ground Laws: Civil

Rights and Public Safety Implications of the Expanded Use of Deadly Force," and both Georgia and Florida state legislature committee hearings for the repeal of the Stand Your Ground law. Lucia recently retired from Delta Airlines in-flight service after thirty years. She received her bachelor of arts degree in political science from Virginia State University and is a member of Delta Sigma Theta Sorority, Inc.

DR. CARLISS McGHEE

Carliss is the proud co-owner of Khocolate Keepsakes Children's Literacy Museum, a facility dedicated to promoting reading among inner-city children. She earned her doctorate in prenatal and perinatal psychology and is the author of five children's books. Carliss was elected to the Inglewood Unified School District in 2013, and she currently serves as its president. She is a member of Delta Sigma Theta Sorority, Inc., and resides in Los Angeles with her family.

REV. MIRIAM MÉNDEZ

Miriam has served in pastoral ministry for more than eighteen years in both English- and Spanish-speaking congregations. She has planted two churches: a team-based, multidenominational church plant in southwest Portland, Oregon; and a bilingual beloved community, Esperanza Church, in southeast Portland. She is a spiritual director with more than fifteen years of experience. Most recently, Miriam served as the associate executive minister for the American Baptist Churches of the Central Pacific Coast (Oregon and Northern California). Her passion and work for justice, diversity, mission, and the health and spiritual wholeness of churches and leaders has led her to serve on the board of directors of the American Baptist Home Mission Societies, the board of directors of the Oregon Latino Action Agenda, the ABCUSA Ministers Council Personal and Spiritual Wholeness Team, and the American Baptist Women in Ministry Advisory Team.

REVEREND DR. GLORIA E. MILLER

Gloria is an associate pastor at First Baptist Church of Glenarden and a proud African American. She is a graduate of Trinity College in Washington, D.C., where she served as the first Protestant chaplain. She holds a master of divinity degree from Howard University School of Divinity. In 2013, she earned a Doctor of ministry degree from Regent University in Virginia Beach, Virginia, graduating summa cum laude. From 1999 to 2000, she served as chief of staff and senior assistant at Metropolitan Baptist Church in Washington, D.C. Since 2002, she has served as associate pastor at the First Baptist Church of Glenarden in Landover, Maryland.

AYANNA MISHOE-BROOKER

Ayanna is the proud daughter of Mr. and Mrs. Luna I. Mishoe and the wife of Reverend Johnnie D. Brooker Jr., pastor of Mt. Zion Baptist Church in Dover, N.J. They have one son, Johnnie Elisha, and one daughter, Annaya Kai. In 2007, Ayanna became the leading lady of Mt. Zion Baptist Church. In 2011, she was licensed to preach the gospel. She received her master of divinity degree in pastoral leadership from the Andersonville Theological Seminary in April 2014. She has preached at numerous retreats and revivals and has taught at several workshops and conferences. Ayanna enjoys encouraging people of all ages to reach their fullest potential and to utilize the Holy Spirit with which God has endowed them. She also enjoys and is committed to praying for others, visiting the shut-in, providing for those in need, mentoring high school students in the Eagle Flight Squadron, and volunteering at the St. Barnabas Medical Center neonatal intensive care unit on a regular basis.

KENYA L. MOORE (LADY K)

Lady K is a native of Hyattsville, Maryland. She is a graduate of Johnson C. Smith University in Charlotte, North Carolina, where she earned a bachelor's degree in social work, and the University of Pennsylvania in Philadelphia, where she earned a master's in social work. Lady K is a motivational speaker, minister, mentor for young ladies, and parent educator. She is the founder of Unveil the Mask Discover the Divine You, which has afforded her the opportunity to compose a CD and develop a YouTube channel featuring "Encouraging Encounters" videos to motivate others. She is unconditionally married to her partner in ministry, Pastor John A. Moore III. Lady K is a proud member of Alpha Kappa Alpha Sorority, Inc.

ELIZABETH MURRAY
Elizabeth is a proud Black woman born in Harlem, New York (April 1, 1940), and a mother of two sons, seven grandchildren, and seven great-granddaughters. A retired bank officer, she is enjoying the best sixteen years of her adult life. She spends her time traveling, bowling, dancing, reading, painting ceramics, volunteering, and serving God. She is a lover of jazz and classical music, in which she fondly engaged during her years at the High School of Music and Art, playing the piano and violin. A magna cum laude graduate of Fordham University with a bachelor of business administration, she applied all her knowledge to developing a fruitful, exciting, joyous, and above all adventurous life. Lady Liz does it her way!

MERCEDES NESFIELD
Mercedes is a retired educator for the New York City School District. A faithful member of Canaan Baptist Church of Christ, she enjoys book clubs, crossword puzzles, jazz, R&B and gospel music, and watching and playing tennis.

PAMELA PALANQUE-NORTH
Pamela has more than twenty-five years of experience as an innovator in the fields of organization development, training and education, and leadership development. She holds advanced degrees from the New School for Social Research in New York City, as well as a profes-

sional certificate in industrial and organization psychology from the Yale University School of Medicine Division for Training and Consultation. She lives in New York with her husband, Robert J. North, a professor of dentistry at Columbia University and Harlem Hospital; their daughters, Blaine and Maegan; and their extraordinary grandson, Judah Manuel Turnbull. Pamela has served as a manager and evaluator for organization development training programs at Yale University's Division for Training and Consultation; principal investigator at New York University Medical Center, Urban Health Affairs; director of training and education at the Institute for Puerto Rican Urban Studies; and senior internal organization effectiveness consultant at AT&T, Bell Laboratories. She believes that a key ingredient to successful inter-cultural interactions is commitment to understanding the language, ways, and customs of others, as well as having a sincere regard and respect for others.

PHYLLIS PORCHER
Phyllis resides in Queens, New York, with her two daughters and husband. She was reared in North Carolina in the Presbyterian Church, and was later baptized by Dr. Johnson Cook into the Baptist Church. She is a crafter and is employed at Queens Library, where she also teaches knitting classes.

DR. MARJORIE DUNCAN REED
Marjorie is a native Pennsylvanian of African American descent, and holds master of theology and Doctor of ministry degrees from Slidell Baptist Seminary in Slidell, Louisiana. She is pastor of St. Paul's Baptist Church in Conshohocken, Pennsylvania, and the first woman to serve as second vice moderator of the Suburban Baptist Association of Southeastern Pennsylvania. She is a hospice chaplain at Abington Memorial Hospital and a member of the Black Clergy of Philadelphia; Baptist Pastors and Ministers Conference of Philadelphia Baptist Clergy Women; and Genesis Ministers Conference. For the past

sixteen years she has served on the board of directors for the Merck Sharp & Dohme Federal Credit Union.

KIM MARTIN SADLER

Kim is president of Sadler Communications & Consulting Group. She is the former editorial director of the Pilgrim Press and the first lady of Mt. Zion Congregational Church, United Church of Christ in Cleveland, Ohio. Kim and her husband, the Reverend Paul Hobson Sadler Sr., have been married for thirty-four years.

MINISTER ANNA P. SHANKLIN, PH.D.

Anna is a native of Baton Rouge, Louisiana, on a mission to win souls for an equal-opportunity God. She is the first female to be officially licensed to the Gospel ministry in the 139-year history of First Missionary Baptist Church of Frederick, Maryland. She is the founder and president of In the Fold Ministries, an urban global ministry based in Atlanta, created in accordance with John 10:16 and Luke 4:18–19. In the Fold has as its purpose to support and execute the mission and preach and teach the Gospel of Jesus Christ. The ministry is dedicated to seeking and sustaining sheep for the Good Shepherd.

REVEREND MARY SHEFFIELD

Mary is a proud African American and native Detroiter with a dedicated track record of service and leadership. She is a bachelor of arts graduate of Wayne State University, where she also earned a master's degree in public administration. Called to preach at age sixteen, she is an ordained minister active in her mission. In November 2013, Mary became the youngest member ever elected to the Detroit City Council, at age twenty-six, and is currently serving a four-year term.

LYNN SPIVEY

Lynn is a business leader and civil rights activist. She hosts a weekly radio show, *Let Your Voice Be Heard*, and serves as president of the

National Association for the Advancement of Colored People (NAACP) New York City Housing Authority Branch. Lynn holds a master's degree in public administration. She is a member of Delta Sigma Theta Sorority, Inc., and serves as the chair of the board for the African American International Chamber of Commerce.

JOANN STEVENS

Joann is a communications strategist, program producer, and writer residing in Washington, D.C. A former *Washington Post* writer and PR strategist, she has promoted issues on higher education reform, diversity in corporate America, and jazz as America's original music. She is coauthor of *In Goode Faith* (Judson Press, 1992), the autobiography of Philadelphia's first Black mayor; and a contributor to *Sister to Sister: Devotions for and from African American Women*, Vol. 1 (Judson Press, 1995).

REVEREND DR. RUTH TRAVIS

Ruth is the first female pastor of Ebenezer African Methodist Episcopal Church in Baltimore. She received her bachelor of science degree in physical education from Morgan State University; master of education degree from West Chester University; and her master's degree in theology from St. Mary's Seminary in Baltimore. In May 1992, Dr. Travis received her Doctor of ministry degree from the United Theological Seminary in Dayton, Ohio.

REVEREND DR. JOAN L. WHARTON

Joan has blazed a trail that conveys bravery—as a church developer and pastor with a clearly articulated vision and a willingness to take risks—that has produced meaningful and relevant ministry. Her brilliance as an entrepreneur suggests a passion and fervor for women, girls, and their particular and unique concerns. She balances life as an author, revivalist, facilitator, and teacher who communicates a strong character and compassionate spirit. Joan also serves as the senior pastor of Hemingway Temple AME Church in Baltimore, executive director of One Church, One Child of Maryland, and founder of Seasoned Women Ministries.

DONNA WHITE

Donna is a New York City real estate professional who is transitioning into her next career as a health and wellness writer, educator, and speaker. Born and raised in the New York area, she currently lives in Manhattan with her husband of almost thirty years, Charles White, and their two children, Justin and Jordan. Donna is proud and happy to be part of a dynamic and nurturing community of women, and looks forward to continuing her close relationships with her beloved sisters.

MICHELE WILLIAMS

Michele is excited and amazed to walk in her own shoes as an educated, smart, and beautiful African American woman of God. As president of the very first full-service casting and talent agency in Georgia, Atlanta Casting and Talent, she has been gifted as a speaker, radio personality, television host, writer, director, producer, award-winning playwright, hat designer, and yes, a cook! Her plays have covered a multitude of subjects in Black history, drama, nonfiction, and comedy. An anointed minister with spirit-filled gifts, she is also a wife, mother of five (ages thirteen to thirty-three), and grandmother of four (ages five to eight) who always has time to connect with those in need. She now truly understands the will of God for her life and what He means in the call of the "virtuous woman" (Proverbs 31).

TERRY B. WILLIAMS

Terry B. Williams, formerly of Bennettsville, South Carolina, now resides in Brooklyn, New York, where she is a civilian employee of the

New York Police Department. She is cofounder of Tradition, an organization that helps seniors. A graduate of Cornell University's Union women's studies program and Hunter College, she received a bachelor's degree in political science. Terry was also an intern with former congresswoman Shirley Chisholm.

More from Ambassador Suzan Johnson Cook . . .

Becoming a Woman of Destiny:
Turning Life's Trials into Triumphs!

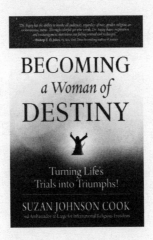

With timeless biblical principles as a foundation, as well as transformative modern-day examples, Ambassador "Sujay" illustrates that every woman is destined for a remarkable life. In *Becoming a Woman of Destiny*, she explains how women can release themselves from their prisons of fear, failure, and a painful past, and move forward confidently into their own greatness. Also included in this life-changing book are guidelines for creating Destiny Circles—powerful groups of women who come together for support, inspiration, and encouragement.